AN INTRODUCTION TO
GREAT ARTISTS

MANET   *Collection Rouart, Paris*

MONSIEUR AND MADAME AUGUSTE MANET
Portrait by Manet of his parents. This was exhibited at the Salon of 1861.

AN INTRODUCTION TO

GREAT ARTISTS

MARY FORRESTER

BLANDFORD PRESS

LONDON

© 1965 BLANDFORD PRESS LTD
167 High Holborn, London, W.C.I.

DEDICATION

To Eironwen who shared the delights of Florence and Rome

AUTHOR'S NOTE

The idea for this book was born during visits to Florence and Rome, to the monastery of S. Marco, the Uffizi Gallery, and the Sistine Chapel. The aim is to give to young people an idea of the heritage of art in Europe and to introduce them to the great masters who have left this priceless legacy.

I should like to thank Miss Barbara Hill, an artist and art teacher, for help and advice, and to acknowledge my gratitude to the late Mr. Charles Johnson and to Mrs. E. M. King for their inspiring lectures.

M. F.

PRINTED IN HOLLAND BY THE YSEL PRESS

CONTENTS

GIOTTO   THE MIRACLE OF THE SPRING

A fresco in the Church of St Francis, Assisi, of about 1296-99

I

Friend of Saint Francis

GIOTTO

In the fourth century A.D. during the reign of Constantine, the first Christian Emperor, the capital of the Roman Empire was moved from Rome to Byzantium in Asia Minor. This city later became Constantinople and is now Istanbul, one of the great cities of Turkey. Christian churches were built there, the greatest of which was St Sophia, and these were decorated by Byzantine artists. Their pictures, though beautiful in colour and painted in a devout spirit, were designed rather mechanically as flat patterns against gold backgrounds with stiff, wooden figures and little or no attempt to suggest space or movement. Often pictures were made in the medium of mosaic—coloured cubes of stone or glass fitted together. The effect was brilliant but inclined to be lifeless and lacking in human interest.

The Byzantine style spread to Italy, the country in which European painting had its birth, and the churches of Ravenna contain wonderful examples of mosaic work. In those early centuries the only patron of art was the Church. It dictated not only the subject matter of pictures, but even the way in which they were to be painted, leaving the artist no initiative. It is not surprising therefore that, up to the fourteenth century, decorations were often formal and monotonous.

In Rome, however, another influence helped to mould the style of those painters who tried to introduce more individuality into their work. The early Christians hiding in the catacombs under the city employed some of their time in making drawings on the walls. Hastily done by untrained men, these sketches often show more warmth and humanity, especially in the portrayal of Christ, than the more formal Byzantine work.

About the year 1182 there was born in the town of Assisi a man who had a profound effect on the whole religious life of Italy. This was St Francis, son of a rich merchant, the saint who gave up all his wealth to devote his life to God; who loved all living things and called them his brothers and sisters. About 1210 he founded the order of wandering friars called Franciscans just about the same time as another great saint, St Dominic, founded the Dominican Order. Both orders still exist to-day.

When St Francis died, he was buried at Assisi and a two-storied church was built over his grave. Famous artists of the time were commissioned to decorate the upper and lower churches of St Francesco and among them was Giotto di Bondone, the first of the great painters of Florence.

Although Giotto was an important figure in his own day and a friend of Italy's two great writers, Dante and Petrarch, very little is known about his life. Even the date of his birth is uncertain, but he is thought to have been born near Florence between 1267 and 1276. It is not known who his parents were; some historians think they were shepherd folk, others that he came of a well-to-do family. There is a legend that Cimabue, one of the foremost painters of the time, came upon Giotto, a shepherd boy, carving a picture of a sheep on a rock and took him to his studio, where he was trained as an artist. Be that as it may, Giotto certainly introduced country scenes into some of his pictures. Modern historians think it likely that his teacher was not Cimabue, but Cavallini, an artist who worked chiefly in Rome. Giotto himself is known to have visited Rome where he almost certainly saw the drawings in the catacombs.

One of Giotto's first tasks was to help in the decoration of the upper church of St Francesco at Assisi, by painting frescoes on the walls to illustrate scenes in the life of St Francis. Although the pictures are now in poor condition and not all of them are by the hand of Giotto, enough of his work remains to show that he was developing a more individual style than that of his predecessors. His figures are no longer flat patterns on the surface of the picture, but human beings moving about in space. He was an architect as well as a painter, and used buildings as part of his compositions; in fact in the scene called "Christmas Night in Greccio" he placed his actors inside a church where St Francis is blessing the Christ child in a manger. He attempted to paint realistic backgrounds of rocks and hills and he introduced trees, animals and birds into his scenes, as in the delightful "Sermon to the Birds", one of the best known of the Assisi frescoes (p. 14) and in "Miracle of the Spring" (p. 6).

Giotto's finest work is at Padua, in Santa Maria dell' Arena, the church which was built on the site of a Roman arena or amphitheatre.

GIOTTO   *Santa Maria dell' Arena, Padua*

THE LAST JUDGMENT

In the year 1300 Enrico Scrovegni, a wealthy citizen of Padua, presented a new chapel to Santa Maria. Dante, the great poet, author of the *Inferno,* is said to have suggested that Giotto should paint a "Last Judgment" at the end of the chapel, which he did. He introduced into it a portrait of Scrovegni presenting a model of his chapel to the Virgin Mary. Giotto was also commissioned to paint over thirty frescoes for the walls.

Giotto's feelings can be imagined as he stood in the new building with its vaulting of blue and gold and its bare brick walls, ready to be primed with the damp plaster on which he would have to paint his frescoes or "fresh" pictures rapidly before it was dry. In Assisi he was one of several artists working on the frescoes, but here on these bare and empty walls he realised the great opportunity of his life.

Giotto was a man of deep religious feeling, and also a great storyteller. He chose as his theme the life of the Virgin Mary and the life of Christ. The series begins with the story of Joachim and Anna, Mary's parents. The elderly couple longed for a child, but when Joachim went to the Temple to offer a sacrifice it was refused and he went sadly into the wilderness. There an angel appeared to him in a dream prophesying the birth of a daughter, while at the same time another angel announced the birth to Anna. Joyfully Joachim and Anna met and embraced at the Golden Gate of Jerusalem. The story continues with the Birth of Mary, her Presentation in the Temple, her Marriage to Joseph and other incidents. "The Wedding Procession of the Virgin" is memorable for the musicians playing on violin and flute.

This leads on to Christ's Nativity, the Adoration of the Kings, and scenes from the New Testament, such as the Marriage at Cana and the Raising of Lazarus, culminating in the Entry into Jerusalem, the Crucifixion and the appearance to Mary Magdalene after the Resurrection.

All the frescoes are nobly conceived and superbly executed. Two of the most famous of the earlier ones are "Joachim Taking Refuge Among the Shepherds" (p. 11) and "Joachim's Dream", where the old man sits hunched up asleep, his head on his knees, in front of the sheepfold, and the angel comes flying down from heaven.

Perhaps the most beautiful of the scenes from the life of Christ is "The Entry into Jerusalem". The composition is carefully planned: Christ riding the ass occupies the centre of the picture, on one side behind him the disciples are grouped, and in front are the people of Jerusalem coming out to greet him.

There is original treatment, too, in "Christ and Mary Magdalene". Christ is on the extreme right, and Mary kneels before him. The rest of the composition consists of the tomb guarded by two very solid angels, while at its foot four Roman soldiers lie asleep.

Giotto began his work in the chapel in 1303 and finished it two years later. The frescoes, though not in perfect condition, are in a better state of preservation than most of his other work, and a study of them will

GIOTTO   *Santa Maria dell' Arena, Padua*

JOACHIM TAKING REFUGE AMONG THE SHEPHERDS

Joachim, a dignified figure, walks with bowed head towards the pitying shepherds.

show how much originality and skill the artist possessed, in spite of restrictions, both in his choice of subject matter and in the manner of presenting it.

Byzantine influence can still be seen in the slant-eyed Eastern faces and the thick gold of the haloes, but there is a break with tradition in the paintings of blue backgrounds rather than the usual gold. The colours are delicately blended, although fresco painting does not allow the sparkling brilliance of mosaic work or the sharp contrasts possible in painting on wood.

Giotto's training as an architect must have helped him immensely in arranging his compositions and in his presentation of buildings such as the golden gate of Jerusalem with its arch and brickwork, and the walls and door of the room in "The Marriage at Cana".

Although the laws of perspective were not properly understood in his day, he began to introduce landscape backgrounds of rocks and trees in outdoor scenes such as "Joachim Taking Refuge Among the Shepherds" and "The Flight into Egypt". The beautiful, delicate tracery of trees and flowers is an important part of the decoration in "The Entry into Jerusalem" and "Christ and Mary Magdalene".

Giotto's painting of animals often shows a somewhat primitive knowledge of anatomy but is none the less charming for this naivety. Nobody has ever seen sheep quite like those in the sheepfold where Joachim seeks refuge, nor a camel like the one that stands open-mouthed in astonishment in the "Adoration of the Kings"; on the other hand the dog who greets Joachim is painted with an enormous amount of sympathy and so is the donkey which forms an important part of the composition in "The Flight into Egypt" (opposite).

Giotto gives his human beings a solidity which is almost sculptural. Joachim has a dignity, the Virgin Many a serenity and Christ a nobility which is in violent contrast to the stupid, brutish face of Judas as he betrays him with a kiss (p. 15).

Giotto must have been inspired as he painted these pictures, for these scenes have never been represented with more sensitivity.

After the completion of the Padua series, Giotto painted three sets of frescoes for the church of Santa Croce or the Holy Cross in Florence. One series portrayed scenes in the life of St John the Baptist and another dealt with St John the Evangelist.

Frescoes are more liable to deterioration than other pictures, as they cannot easily be removed from the walls on which they are painted,

GIOTTO   *Santa Maria dell' Arena, Padua*
ADORATION OF THE KINGS

GIOTTO   *Santa Maria dell' Arena, Padua*
THE FLIGHT INTO EGYPT

GIOTTO   *Church of St. Francis, Assisi*

THE SERMON TO THE BIRDS

St Francis holds out his hands to the birds as he addresses them.

GIOTTO   *Santa Maria dell' Arena, Padua*

THE BETRAYAL OF CHRIST

Detail of the faces of Christ and Judas. The nobility of Jesus contrasts with the stupid,
brutish face of Judas who betrays Him with a kiss.

and unfortunately both these series are in bad condition, but they are being restored at the present time.

In his third series Giotto returned once again to the life of St Francis. Although the pictures have been altered and over-painted, it is interesting to compare them with the earlier ones at Assisi and to note how Giotto has developed in his ability to manage compositions containing many figures. The most famous in this series is "The Funeral of St Francis", in which the saint, a dignified figure, lies on a bier surrounded by mourning friars.

In the Uffizi Gallery in Florence a "Madonna and Child with Angels" by Cimabue, Giotto's predecessor, is placed near a picture of the same subject by Giotto. As a piece of decoration the Cimabue is beautiful, a piece of flat patterning with little body or substance. Giotto's Madonna, on the other hand, is a grand monumental figure who appears to be really sitting on her throne, with the child firmly perched on her knee and the angels looking at her in adoration. The altarpiece was painted by Giotto for the church of the Ognissanti in Florence, This is a painting on wood and so it is the best preserved of all his pictures.

Giotto is known to have painted in Naples and in Rimini, but all these pictures are lost. One of his achievements was a large mosaic for the old church of St Peter's in Rome called the "Navicella", illustrating the story of St Peter walking on the sea, while the other disciples watch from the deck of a ship. This is still over the porch in St Peter's, but it has been so altered and disfigured that it is no longer recognizable as the work of Giotto.

In 1334 Giotto was appointed City Architect of Florence. He started to design the rectangular bell-tower or Campanile of the Cathedral, but this was unfinished when he died in 1337.

The importance of Giotto's contribution to Italian painting cannot be exaggerated. He was the first to teach that art belonged not only to the Church but also to the people. He had many followers and imitators known as "The Giotteschi", and his work was the first step towards the great flowering of Italian art in the Renaissance. It is surely not fanciful to conclude that he was imbued with the spirit of the great saint whose life he portrayed, and, as he surveyed his achievements, he might have murmured in the very words of St Francis, "Praise ye and bless ye the Lord and give thanks unto him and serve him with humility".

2

The Monk of San Marco

FRA ANGELICO

In the year 1437 Cosimo I, the ruler of Florence, was worried. A member of the wealthy banking family of the Medici, he was feeling twinges of conscience about some rather shady business deals in which he had been engaged. He asked the Pope, who was visiting him at the time, what he could do as a penance, and the Pope suggested that he gave ten thousand gold sovereigns for the decoration of the Dominican monastery at Fiesole near Florence.

Cosimo, a generous man, undertook instead to rebuild the old ruined convent of San Marco in Florence and give it to the Dominicans. He commissioned Michelozzo, one of the foremost architects of the day, to design the new building. It was to be built round a courtyard and to have forty cells for the monks, as well as a meeting hall, dining room and hospice or welcoming room for pilgrims who must never be turned away, no matter at what time of day or night they arrived. There was also to be a large library, for which Cosimo gave some priceless books. It was later used by scholars from all over Italy and in fact became the first public library in Europe.

Among the monks who came to San Marco when the building was finished were two brothers, Fra Benedetto and Fra Giovanni. Benedetto was well known as an illustrator of illuminated manuscripts and Giovanni had been trained in Florence as a painter. He had already painted an altarpiece for St Dominic's church at Fiesole which was so lovely in design and colour that it was known as the work of "Beato Angelico" and the artist has been called Fra or Friar Angelico ever since.

A part of this altarpiece, "Christ Glorified" is in the National Gallery in London. It shows Christ in a white robe, carrying a red and white banner, and its five panels contain about a hundred and fifty figures of saints and angels dressed in exquisite robes of blue and green and red, with haloes painted in gold leaf, and set against a golden background. Fra Angelico must have studied closely the beautiful illuminated

FRA ANGELICO   *San Marco, Florence*

THE FLIGHT INTO EGYPT

One of several small panel pictures representing scenes from the life of Christ. They are
thought to have been painted originally for the doors of a silver chest in the church of S.
Annunziata in Florence.

manuscripts, to the painting of which monks like his brother Benedetto devoted their whole lives.

To Fra Angelico was given the important task of decorating the new monastery with wall-paintings and frescoes. Through Cosimo's generosity he had at his disposal the best and most expensive colours, although he himself was not paid for his work.

The theme of the decoration was the Christian faith, illustrated by scenes from the New Testament. Although the best of the pictures and all the designs were by Fra Angelico himself, he was obliged to make use of pupils and assistants to help in the work.

In every cell there was a picture on which the eyes of the monks could dwell while they meditated on the mysteries of the Christian faith. Among the scenes painted for them were "The Nativity", "The Transformation" and "Christ and Mary Magdalene" ("Noli me Tangere"). In Cosimo's own cell, where he often came to pray, Fra Angelico painted "The Adoration of the Kings", which shows the first king offering his riches to Jesus, as Cosimo himself had done.

As well as the cells, the other rooms in the monastery had to be decorated. For the staircase leading to the cells Fra Angelico painted a very beautiful "Annunciation".

The decoration of San Marco took nine years. By the time it was finished in 1445 Fra Angelico had become so famous that the Pope sent for him to decorate a chapel in the Vatican in Rome. Later he returned to his first monastery at Fiesole and was himself its prior for three years. Then he went back to Rome where he died in 1455. On his tombstone were carved these words: "The city, flower of Tuscany, made me, Giovanni", meaning that his best work was done in Florence.

The life of Fra Angelico was holy and devout. He always prayed before taking up his brush and never altered anything once he had painted it, because he believed that the hand of God guided him in everything he undertook. He felt the tragedy of the Crucifixion so deeply that tears poured down his face while he was painting it. He disliked having to depict the lost souls in the "Last Judgment", but delighted in the dance of the angels in the gardens of Paradise in the same picture. Flowers and rather formal trees add to the beauty of the paintings. The angel of the "Annunciation" steps in from a garden, and there are scenes in the Garden of Gethsemane and the Garden of the Resurrection. The donkey carries Mary and Jesus along a flower-lined path in "The Flight into Egypt".

Much of Fra Angelico's charm lies in his use of colour. The most brilliant effects were obtained in the altarpieces, but the frescoes, though subdued, are equally beautiful.

Fra Angelico was one of the first great decorators of European art. He was influenced by the painting of Byzantium or Constantinople in the East where the Roman Empire under Constantine had its head-quarters for a time. This influence can be seen in the slanting eyes of some of the figures, the gold backgrounds and the painting of the Christ Child not as a solid baby figure, but looking either like a doll or a little grown-up man.

Many years after his death, San Marco became a museum for his works and a number of his pictures were brought from other churches and galleries in Italy to hang in the hospice there, where they can still be seen. Among them was the famous "Madonna and Child" which the linen-weavers of Florence commissioned Fra Angelico to paint for their church and for which they paid one hundred and ninety gold florins to have painted "inside and out with gold, blue and silver of the best and finest that can be found". On the side panels Fra Angelico painted his most famous angels, dressed in beautiful robes of rich green, blue and purple and playing on musical instruments.

Today hundreds of visitors to Italy cross the quiet courtyard of San Marco with its giant cedar tree to marvel at the pictures of the artist who painted only for the glory of God.

DETAIL OF ANGEL
From Madonna
and Child
S. Marco

3

The Mysterious Brothers

THE VAN EYCKS

Flemish painting started in the early years of the fifteenth century in the Netherlands, which then included parts of France and Germany, as well as the countries we now know as Belgium and Holland.

Unlike Italian artists, the first Flemish painters did not come under the influence of Byzantine work from the East. Their style developed from the mediaeval illuminated manuscripts and Books of Hours which were popular at the time.

In studying the work of the van Eycks, the first great artists of the Flemish school, a mystery immediately arises. On the famous altarpiece at Ghent there is an inscription which reads as follows (in translation):

The painter, Hubert van Eyck, than whom none was greater,
began this work which Jan, the second in the art,
completed at the request of Jodocus Vyt.
Friday, 6th May, 1432.

Apart from the inscription and a few rather vague allusions, there is no record of Hubert having painted any pictures; there are certainly none signed by him. Some people think that the inscription is a forgery and even that Hubert never existed. Although there is no proof either way, most authorities agree that Hubert probably did design the Ghent altarpiece and painted some of it.

There are one or two other pictures rather different in style from those known to be Jan's work, which may have been painted by Hubert; for instance, "The Three Marys at the Sepulchre" in Rotterdam, with solid, realistic sleeping soldiers, and an "Annunciation" in Washington It is thought from the copy of a tomb inscription that Hubert died in 1426.

A good deal more is known about the younger brother, Jan, although the date of his birth also is uncertain. In 1422 he was court painter to

Count John of Bavaria and worked on the decoration of his Palace in The Hague. On the death of Count John in 1425 he was appointed court painter and gentleman-in-waiting to Philip the Good, Duke of Burgundy, who ruled over the Netherlands for nearly fifty years. He was so well trusted that the Duke sent him on several diplomatic missions, and also confidential ones. He went to Portugal to make the arrangements for the Duke to marry Isabella, the daughter of the King of Portugal. The portrait he painted of her may have had a part in the successful outcome! It is not known where this portrait is now.

In 1430 Jan van Eyck settled in Bruges. The Duke of Burgundy visited him there to buy one of his pictures. He thought most highly of him, as a man of excellent taste and artistic skill, and this opinion was shared by others who wrote about him at the time.

Perhaps the greatest example of his skill is the altarpiece in the church of St Bavon in Ghent. It is one of the most beautiful works of art, and every year thousands of people come from all parts of the world to see it. Like other pictures commissioned for the Church in the early times, when most of the people could not read, it was designed to express a great religious truth. And the altarpiece has indeed an attraction beyond that of artistic ingenuity and beauty (see p. 26).

The Ghent altarpiece is a polyptych, that is, it is made up of many separate panels, and it has survived many misadventures. It has been damaged by fire, broken up and in the Napoleonic wars some of the panels were stolen. It was not until 1923 that all the lost parts were restored and the altarpiece was again in its entirety at St Bavon. Eleven years later the panel with the Just Judges was stolen, and it is represented there today by a copy.

The Ghent altarpiece is a work of genius, most accomplished for such an early period in European art. The colours have a jewel-like brilliance, seen in the splendid red robes of God the Father and the prophets, the blue of the Virgin's mantle, the rich green of St John's garment and the red and gold of the cloak worn by the singing angel.

It used to be said that the van Eycks invented oil painting; this is now known not to be so but it is probably true that they perfected the technique of oil glazes to make the colours more luminous. They knew too how to produce the effects of light and they understood what is known as air perspective, making the tones less clear as the picture recedes, and objects in the distance, especially hills, appear blue.

Though the faces in Flemish paintings are less ideally beautiful than in many Italian works, they have a spiritual loveliness of their own, very evident in van Eyck's conception of the Virgin and the angels, intent on praise and prayer.

Another characteristic of Flemish pictures is the meticulous attention given to all the small details. In the Ghent altarpiece every fold of the robes, every jewel in the crowns, every flower in the landscape, is fascinatingly portrayed. The music desk of the singing angels is decorated with a tiny, lovely representation of St George killing the dragon, painted to resemble a wood carving. Some touches of everyday life are introduced.

Jan van Eyck painted other important religious pictures, including a splendid altarpiece in Dresden depicting the Virgin and Child with Saints and a Donor. One of his most interesting pictures is in the Municipal Museum at Bruges, "The Madonna and Child with Canon van der Paele". The Madonna sits enthroned with a rich carpet beneath her feet; the solemn old canon, glasses in hand, kneels in adoration, while St George in a suit of armour and another saint, wearing the gorgeous robes of a bishop, look on. In mood it is serene and tranquil, like most of the early Flemish pictures, with no attempt to represent movement or drama. The most fascinating part of "The Madonna and Child with Chancellor Rolin" in the Louvre, is the view through the archway showing two little figures on a parapet gazing at the river winding away into the blue distance over which a bridge carries people to and from the town. Every detail in this beautiful little picture is painted with scrupulous care.

Like many artists of the period, Jan van Eyck painted portraits as well as religious pictures. Most of them have a mystery of some kind attached to them. There is for instance, the "Portrait of a Young Man" in the National Gallery, painted in 1432; the words "Leal souvenir" (faithful remembrance) "Tym." are inscribed on the painting; nobody knows to what they refer. The "Portrait of a Man" wearing a red turban, also in the National Gallery, may possibly be a self-portrait or a portrait of van Eyck's father-in-law. This has the modest inscription with which van Eyck signed several of his works, "Als ixh xan", "as (well as) I can". The most intriguing and famous van Eyck picture, about which much has been written and said is the "The Marriage of Arnolfini". It was, as far as is known, the first full-length portrait group in Europe of people in everyday surroundings. A wedding ceremony appears to be taking place. The bridegroom, a person with unprepossessing features, takes

VAN EYCK

THE MARRIAGE OF ARNOLFINI

the hand of his meek bride; his other hand is raised as if taking a vow. The scene takes place in a bedroom. Overhead hangs a chandelier with one candle lighted in full daylight. At the back, a mirror reflects the bridal couple and two witnesses entering the room. One of these is presumed to be the artist himself, as on the wall there is the inscription "Johannes de eyck fuit hic, 1434" (Jan van Eyck was here).

Technically, this picture is one of the great masterpieces of art. Every small object is observed with van Eyck's usual care, the oranges on the window sill, the shoes on the floor, the chandelier, the mirrors with scenes from the Passion of Christ carved on its frame and the alert little dog, looking as though he could tell the whole story if he were asked. The softness of the fur in Giovanna's robe is beautifully portrayed, and her voluminous dress is painted with supreme skill. The scene is illuminated by the light which falls across the room from the open window.

Van Eyck's portrait of his wife painted in 1439 was one of his last pictures. It is in the Municipal Museum at Bruges. It shows a lady of great firmness and character wearing a strawberry red gown edged with grey fur, her hair neatly rolled into two coils under her white lace headdress.

Jan van Eyck died in 1441, after a short working life. At his death he was working on a tryptych called "The Madonna and Child with Nicholas Maelbeke" for St Martin's Abbey in Ypres. This painting has an interesting history. It was taken from the Abbey when Napoleon invaded Belgium and over the years it had several owners, including a butcher and a tobacco manufacturer. It disappeared for a long while, but in 1965 it turned up in England and it is now in Warwick Castle. It has been cleaned and all the overpainting by other hands removed. It is considered to be one of van Eyck's masterpieces, although he died before he could add the final oil glazes which would have given it the jewel-like brilliance characteristic of his other work.

All Jan van Eyck's pictures were painted in the brief span of ten years. Many excellent Flemish painters followed him, Rogier van der Weyden, Memling, Hugo van der Goes, but none excelled the first great master in spiritual inspiration or in technical skill.

The Altarpiece at Ghent

The theme of this altarpiece is the redemption from original sin by Jesus Christ.

There are twenty-two panels altogether, twelve inside and ten on the outside which can only be seen when the wings are closed. The inner part is arranged in two rows of pictures, of which the most important panel is the central one in the lower tier, "The Adoration of the Lamb", illustrating passages in the Book of Revelation, "Worthy is the Lamb that was slain . . . for the Lamb which is in the midst of the throne shall lead them into living fountains of waters".

The lamb is standing on an altar with blood pouring from its heart into a chalice, while angels kneel around. Behind are two groups of worshippers, holy bishops on the left and holy maidens on the right. The fountain of life stands in front of the altar with apostles, prophets and martyrs grouped on either side. The scene is lit by the rays of the sun falling on green fields, trees and flowering bushes with towered buildings in the background among the hills which in the far distance are blue.

The four side pancls shown great streams of people on the way to worship the Lamb. From the left ride the Just Judges and the Knights of Christ, among whom are possibly portraits of the van Eycks themselves; converging on the scene from the right on foot are holy hermits and pilgrims with the great figure of St Christopher, the patron saint of travellers, towering above the others. In the upper row, above the "Adoration of the Lamb", God the Father is enthroned in glory, a triple crown on his head and another jewelled crown at his feet, between the Virgin and St John the Baptist. On the left of the Virgin are singing angels and on the right of St John, musical angels, the foremost one playing the organ. On the extreme left is Adam and on the right is Eve.

When the wings are closed, more pictures can be seen on the outside of the shutters, at the top, prophets and sibyls, and in the centre, the Annunciation—the Archangel Gabriel foretelling the birth of Jesus to Mary. Between them is an empty room, containing a washing recess and toilet articles.

VAN EYCK *Cathedral of St Bavon, Ghent*

THE MYSTIC LAMB

Detail, lower zone, central panel of the Adoration of the Lamb

In the centre panels beneath, painted in a grey colour called grisaille to resemble marble statues, are two figures. One is of John the Baptist, carrying a lamb. He was the forerunner of Jesus, of whom he said: "Behold the Lamb of God which taketh away the sin of the world." The other figure is of John the Evangelist, whose Revelation was the source of inspiration for "The Adoration of the Lamb".

Also on the outer panels are the devout kneeling figures of Jodocus Vydt, who paid for the altarpiece and gave it to the church, and his wife.

4

Painter of the Golden Age

BOTTICELLI

In 1445, ten years before Fra Angelico died, Mariano Filipepi, the tanner of Florence, had a son whom he named Alessandro. The boy, one of a large family, decided very early in life that he wanted to be a painter. There is a story that he was apprenticed to a goldsmith called Botticelli and that was how he came by his name, but some say it was because one of his brothers who was small and round was called Botticello or "little barrel". At any rate, Sandro Filipepi became the painter we know as Botticelli.

When he was only fifteen, he joined the studio of Fra Filippo Lippi, a famous painter of religious pictures and later he worked with other well-known artists.

It was a joyous time in Florence when Botticelli was a young man. The city was still ruled by the rich merchant family of the Medici; Piero, son of Cosimo I, died in 1469 and was succeeded by his son Lorenzo called "The Magnificent" because he lived in great splendour. He was a young man who enjoyed himself and liked others to do the same, so there were tournaments, processions and pageants nearly every day in the city. But Lorenzo was not a mere playboy, he was a shrewd politician, and was also interested in art, music and literature—in fact he was quite a good poet himself. He gathered round him all the best artists and writers and they used to meet in one or other of the royal palaces or villas to discuss their work and ideas and perhaps to read their poetry and show their pictures. This was the beginning of what was called the Renaissance, when people took a new interest in the old Greek and Roman learning and art. New buildings were designed with classical pillars, decorators and painters illustrated Greek and Roman legends and stories and poets wrote verses in Latin and Greek.

The work of the modest and shy young painter, Botticelli, soon became known in the Medici circle. One of his early masterpieces was an "Adoration of the Magi" painted for the church of Santa Maria Novella, in which some of the figures were Medici portraits.

BOTTICELLI   *National Gallery, London*

THE MYSTIC NATIVITY

Underneath is an inscription in Greek, which reads:

'I, Sandro painted this picture at the end of the year 1500 in the troubles of Italy...according
to the 11th chapter of St John (Revelation)...in the loosing of the Devil for 3 ¼ years then he
will be chained...we shall see...as in this picture'.

No artist has ever been able to paint beautiful dancing figures more gracefully than Botticelli. For one of Lorenzo's relatives he painted two of his most famous pictures to illustrate popular Roman legends. One was called "Primavera" (Spring) and it shows Venus and her nymphs dancing in an orange grove, while Cupid shoots his darts from above. It seems to express the very spirit of springtime. The other, even better known, is "The Birth of Venus". The beautiful golden-haired goddess is being wafted from the sea on a conch shell by the wind spirits, while Spring, a lovely graceful figure, is waiting to throw a cloak around her.

These pictures are now in the Botticelli room at the Uffizi Gallery.

BOTTICELLI   *National Gallery, London*

HEAD OF VENUS

Detail from Venus and Mars

In the National Gallery, London, is "Venus and Mars", which was probably painted as a decoration for a chest or bedhead for one of the rich Florentine families. This Venus is very beautiful, too, as can be seen from the illustration. In the picture there are delightful little satyrs playing with the armour of the sleeping Mars.

Botticelli, like Fra Angelico, was sent by the Pope to work in Rome. He painted three frescoes of scenes in the life of Moses and the life of Christ for the walls of the Sistine Chapel in the Vatican. When he came back to Florence so many commissions were pouring in, especially for Madonna and Child pictures, that he had to open a workshop to deal with them all. Many were by his own hand but others are labelled "School of Botticelli".

There is great sadness in many of Botticelli's beautiful faces, even in happy pictures like "Primavera" and "The Birth of Venus". He seems to be echoing the words in one of Lorenzo's poems:

"Who would be glad then let him be,
Of to-morrow there's no certainty."

In the most haunting of all his Madonna pictures, the "Madonna of the Pomegranate", the Madonna is almost weeping and the child is lifting his hand as if to wave goodbye. Indeed troubles were soon to come thick and fast upon Florence.

It was an age of corruption as well as of splendour; there was weakness within and attacks from without. The Prior of the San Marco monastery at this time, a dark, fiery monk called Savonarola, fought against the depravity of the day and made many enemies. He was finally arrested, tortured and put to death in 1498, six years after the death of Lorenzo the Magnificent.

Botticelli was greatly influenced by Savonarola's teaching, though he may not have been one of his followers. His later works are more sincerely religious than the earlier ones. His "Crucifixion" which is now in America shows the city of Florence, with its cathedral in the background, being punished by God. His last picture, painted in 1500, is in the National Gallery. It is called "Mystic Nativity" and a reproduction is given on page 29.

For the last ten years of his life Botticelli was crippled with paralysis and he had to give up painting altogether. He died in 1510 while German, French and Spanish armies were hammering at the gates of Florence. The golden age of Lorenzo de Medici was over, but it still lives on in the lovely paintings of Sandro Botticelli.

DA VINCI

Louvre, Paris

MONA LISA

5

A Man of Many Parts

LEONARDO DA VINCI

Artist, sculptor, designer, engineer, Leonardo da Vinci, the son of a lawyer, was born in a little village in Northern Italy more than five hundred years ago.

About the same time that Botticelli was studying in Florence, the young Leonardo joined the studio of Verrocchio to learn painting and sculpture. He was a strong, handsome boy with a kind and sensitive nature. He loved flowers and animals, and there is a story that when he walked through the market place of Florence he used to buy wild birds in cages in order to set them free.

In Leonardo's time, pictures were almost always painted either for the Church or for the heads of wealthy families who wanted portraits of themselves and their families. Leonardo, like Botticelli, soon found rich patrons of this kind. But he was not content just to provide beautiful decorations; he wanted to try out experiments in colour, in contrasts of light and shade and in developing a new technique which gave a soft misty atmosphere to his backgrounds. Whether he was painting flowers, animals, rocks or people, he tried to make them as lifelike as possible, while at the same time touching them with a strange beauty.

In Verrocchio's picture "The Baptism of Christ" there is an angel with a beautiful face and long curling hair, which was almost certainly one of the first works of his pupil Leonardo, who was fond of making drawings of hair. In an early work now in Russia called "The Benois Madonna", after someone who once owned it, Leonardo has made the Madonna an ordinary young girl with a fat baby who is staring fixedly at a flower in his hand in the way babies do. He had evidently been making a study of babies!

Like many geniuses, Leonardo was erratic in his work, leaving pictures unfinished, taking years to fulfil orders for which he had been paid, and experimenting so much with new kinds of paint that colours faded and pictures were spoilt even in his own lifetime.

It is interesting to compare Leonardo's "Adoration of the Magi" in the Uffizi Gallery with Botticelli's, painted a few years earlier. Gone are the clear bright colours and the graceful portrait figures; only the brown underpainting has been completed and many of the figures are only sketches. But the mysterious twilight scene is full of action. The child leans forward to touch the gold cup in the king's hand; strange beautiful faces and rearing horses can be faintly seen in the misty background. Much is left to the imagination. We feel that to have added more would only have spoilt the effect.

Leonardo was interested in everything, always studying and experimenting in order to find out what made things work. Among the subjects he mastered were astronomy, botany and engineering. Centuries before the invention of aeroplanes he designed a flying machine which could have been made to work. He made thousands of sketches and drawings showing careful study of engineering, the anatomy of plants and animals, the formation of rocks and the movement of water. Many of these fascinating drawings are in the Queen's Collections at Buckingham Palace and Windsor Castle, and they are often on exhibition to the public.

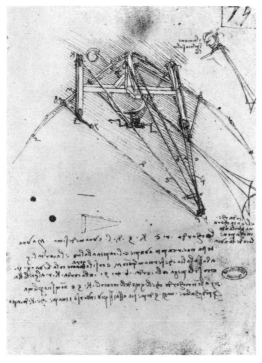

DESIGN FOR A FLYING MACHINE

LEONARDO DA VINCI

Science Museum, Kensington

Leonardo worked for a few years in Florence for Lorenzo the Magnificent. In 1482 Lorenzo wished to give a lute as a present to Ludovico Sforza, Duke of Milan, and he sent Leonardo to present it. In addition to his other talents the young artist was an accomplished musician and the story goes that he played the lute so charmingly that the Duke asked him to stay in Milan. He did in fact stay and was commissioned to carve a huge statue of the Duke on horseback. But he only got as far as making a clay model of the horse, which no longer exists; all that remains is a series of drawings.

In the refectory of the Church of Santa Maria delle Grazie in Milan, Leonardo's masterpiece "The Last Supper", which he painted for the monks, still hangs. This was the picture which soon faded and decayed and was then so much overpainted that little of Leonardo's original work could be seen. But it has recently been carefully cleaned and restored to something like its early beauty.

The subject of "The Last Supper" was a favourite one with Italian painters of this period, who usually showed the disciples sitting quietly at the table. Leonardo's approach is quite different. He places the scene in a real room and leads the eye from the table to the country scene outside the window. Everything is carefully planned, even to the stripes on the tablecloth. At the table, all is movement. It is almost possible to hear the buzz of conversation as the disciples lean over to ask each other the meaning of the strange words they have just heard. But there is order in the arrangement of the figures—a hand outstretched here—a finger pointing upwards there—and the quiet figure of Christ in the middle in contrast to the agitated groups on either side.

Leonardo was too restless to settle in Milan and by 1502 he was back in Florence, painting a portrait of the wife of Francesco del Giocondo. In order to make the lady look relaxed and happy it is said that he ordered clowns and musicians to entertain her while he painted. The result is the "Mona Lisa" with her famous smile which nobody has ever quite been able to understand. (p. 32) She hangs now in the Louvre. Her adventures have included being stolen by a workman in 1911 and a trip to America. The portrait is lovely, with its delicate painting of hair and hands on Leonardo's favourite background of rocks and water.

The strange, fascinating story of Leonardo continues with his two paintings called "The Virgin of the Rocks". How he came to undertake two pictures so much alike is something of a mystery, but there is an explanation which seems to fit in with the facts.

In 1483, while Leonardo was working in Milan, he was asked by the monks of the Immaculate Conception to paint an altarpiece for their church, where it was eventually hung. It is thought that when the King of France invaded Italy he stole the picture and took it to France. It is now in the Louvre. In 1493 Leonardo was commissioned to replace the stolen picture by another as like it as possible, and he painted the second version with the help of pupils. Owing to a lawsuit over payment it was not finished until 1506. Many years later it seems to have been sold and brought to England, and now hangs in the National Gallery.

Both pictures show the Virgin and Child with the little St John the Baptist and an angel sitting in a cavern near a pool with rocks overhead and sticking up out of the water behind. Gaps in the rocks let in the light. The pictures show very well Leonardo's new technique of violent contrasts between light and shadow which came to be called "chiaroscuro". The prevailing colour is a mysterious dark blue with a misty background. In the Louvre picture the Virgin is younger and the children more attractive, the Christ child being particularly beautiful. There are more flowers and the colour is brighter than in the National Gallery version, which has faded considerably. But the angel in the London picture is one of the loveliest things that Leonardo, or any one else, ever painted, with her sweet, wistful expression and exquisite hair. Both pictures have the unworldly, mysterious quality so typical of Leonardo.

All his life Leonardo went on experimenting and trying out various scientific ideas. Once he worked for the famous (or infamous) Cesare Borgia, as a military engineer, designing bridges for his conquering army. It was impossible to realize all his dreams and, as he got older, he became more impatient and frustrated. When the king of France invited him to leave Italy he was glad to go.

In France he continued his scientific and engineering designs and painted his last picture "The Virgin and Child with St. Anne", now in the Louvre. He had earlier made cartoons or drawings for this picture, some of which do not bear much resemblance to the finished work. One of these cartoons, a charcoal drawing on brown paper, became the property of the Royal Academy in London. In 1960 it was decided to sell it in order to raise funds for the Academy schools. Offers of up to a million pounds were received, but there was great opposition to its leaving the country and a fund was opened to buy it for the nation. The National Gallery finally bought it for £800,000, much of it given by

DA VINCI
THE VIRGIN AND
CHILD WITH ST ANNE
(CARTOON)
National Gallery, London

many people throughout the land, and it is now on view in the Gallery.

In the finished picture St Anne, her arms round the Child who is holding a lamb, sits on the Madonna's knee, against a background of Leonardo's favourite rocks and pools. In the cartoon the arrangement is a little different, as can be seen from the illustration. It is a picture of haunting beauty and the fact that so large a sum was willingly subscribed to buy it pays tribute to the work of an artist of whom the great critic, Bernard Berenson, said "Nothing that he touched but turned into a thing of eternal beauty".

Leonardo died from a stroke in 1519 at Choux in France. A self-portrait shows him as a handsome bearded old man, obviously keeping to the end the eager mind and keen intelligence which enabled him to contribute so much to the knowledge and culture of his time.

6

The Goldsmith's Son of Nuremberg

DÜRER

In the year 1455 Albrecht Dürer, a goldsmith of Hungarian extraction, came to take up his calling in the Bavarian city of Nuremberg. Thirteen years later he married the daughter of his teacher, and in 1471 the second of their eighteen children, Albrecht, was born.

Young Albrecht made up his mind that he wanted to be an artist and after serving an apprenticeship with his father, he went at fifteen to study under Michael Wolgemut, a painter and wood designer.

Dürer began his career some years after printing had been invented, about the middle of the fifteenth century. Different methods of reproducing illustrations were also being developed. One of the new techniques was woodcutting in which designs were made by drawing lines on blocks of wood, then cutting away the surrounding parts, inking the lines and pressing them on paper, very much in the way that lino and potato cuts are done to-day. Another method of printing pictures was engraving on copper by making incisions in the metal which were inked in and then rolled on to paper under a heavy press. Dürer used both of these methods; his woodcuts and engravings are as well-known as his paintings. After his apprenticeship, the young artist set out on his "wander years", the time when young men were accustomed to complete their education by travelling abroad. He travelled in Germany and Switzerland. By 1494 he was back in Nuremberg, where he married Agnes Frey, the daughter of a wealthy merchant. They had no children. After his marriage, he paid his first visit to Italy, copying drawings and engravings. He and his wife then settled down to live and work in Nuremberg. There he opened his own workshop, where his desings were carried out.

Germany was in a state of tension and unrest, both political and religious. The Middle Ages were coming to an end, to be replaced by the new ideas and thoughts inspired by the Renaissance or "new birth" in Italy. The invention of printing helped people to increase their knowledge by reading books on all kinds of subjects. Politically, the power of the great emperors was beginning to wane and smaller city states like Nuremberg were becoming centres of culture and learning. Religious life was changing too. The church had become riddled with superstition and during Dürer's lifetime, Martin Luther began to proclaim his ideas of reformation. Dürer was a deeply religious man and although he remained a Catholic, he was influenced by Luther. In addition to the political and religious upheavals, the country was stricken by plague and famine. Many thought the end of the world was near.

All this may have had its effect on one of Dürer's first important works, a set of fifteen woodcuts called "The Apocalypse" produced in 1498 which illustrates the Book of Revelation. These are crowded with figures and full of vigorous movement. Other series of woodcuts followed, including "The Great Passion" and "The Life of the Virgin". "The Small Passion", so called because the woodcuts are much smaller in size than those in "The Great Passion", appeared in 1511. The scenes of Christ's trial and passion are depicted here with deep feeling.

It is interesting to compare Dürer's versions of these religious scenes with those of Giotto or Fra Angelico. The German artist, with down-to-earth realism, imagines the donkey in "The Flight into Egypt" as a large lop-eared animal upon whom Mary rides with her hat strapped to her back, through a forest of pine trees. "The Rest on the Flight" is an even more homely scene as Mary sits at her needlework with the child in a wooden cradle beside her, while Joseph works at his bench, and quaint child angels sweep the shavings into a basket.

Some of Dürer's copperplate engravings are very well known. One of the best is "St Eustace" of about 1500, illustrating the legend of the saint who while out hunting in the forest with his horse and dogs came upon a stag with a crucifix between its horns. The splendid engraving of "The Knight, Death and the Devil" shows a knight in armour riding a horse through a haunted forest and is thought to symbolize the progress of man's soul through life.

Dürer was the first European artist to paint in watercolour and his pictures in this medium are full of atmosphere as well as beautiful in colour. He painted many scenes during his first visit to Italy; one shows the quaint little town of Trento on a sunny day, nestling among lakes and mountains. "The House by the Pond" illustrated on page 43 is as delicate as a Japanese print.

Dürer was a great nature lover. His house in Nuremberg was always crowded with pets, his garden full of flowers. His studies of plants and

animals are among the most pleasing of his watercolours. The life-like picture of a "Young Hare" is in the Albertina Gallery, Vienna, and the exquisite study of a "Squirrel Cracking Nuts" in a Swiss Collection. Two of the best known flower paintings are "The Large Piece of Turf" and "The Small Piece of Turf". Even a modest bunch of violets did not escape his attention.

Animals appear unexpectedly in his religious pictures, for instance in a lovely watercolour "The Virgin and Child with Animals" which includes a parrot and a fox, and a copperplate engraving, "The Virgin and Child with a Monkey", both early works. An engraving of St Jerome shows the saint in his study with his famous lion looking like a large and rather engaging cat.

Dürer left a large number of important drawings, many of them portrait studies. There are several self-portraits, the first a silverpoint of him as a thirteen-year-old schoolboy, and some drawings of his wife Agnes, reputed to have been of a shrewish disposition. Most brilliant of all is a charcoal impression of his mother in 1514, showing her as a sick woman with hollow cheeks and large sunken eyes.

Dürer's formal paintings were few compared with his output of woodcuts and engravings. He started painting portraits early in his career. In the National Gallery is a portrait of his father, painted in 1497. As there are four separate versions of this picture, some critics regard it as a copy, but it is a fine penetrating study of the severe, shrewd and yet likeable old goldsmith.

In the earlier part of his career, Dürer was fond of painting himself; two of the best known self-portraits are the 1498 picture in Madrid and one of 1500 in Munich. Dürer portrays himself with long curling hair flowing on to his shoulders but as it is thought he gave himself the features he would like to have had rather than those he really possessed, these pictures may not be perfect likenesses.

Dürer had many commissions for altarpieces. One of the first, "The Adoration of the Magi", now in the Uffizi Gallery, is well-known and is interesting for the fact that the second king bears a strong likeness to the self portraits the artist was painting at the time. In 1500, Dürer painted an altarpiece for the Paumgartner family. (See page 42.)

In 1505, Dürer paid a second most important visit to Italy and this time he met Giovanni Bellini, the master of Titian. Although he never painted in the oil medium (his technique was the earlier one of egg tempera on wood), he was a great deal influenced by Italian methods of composition. While he was in Venice he was asked to paint a picture for the German Merchants' Exchange, which was later decorated by Giorgione and Titian. He painted "The Festival of the Rose Garlands", so called because the Virgin and Child and St Dominic are crowning Pope Julius 11 and the Emperor Maximilian with roses.

In comparison with the Paumgartner picture, this shows much greater skill in the use of space and the arrangement of the figures. It contains several portraits among the onlookers including one of Dürer himself. It was acquired many years later by the Emperor Rudolf I and men carried it by hand to Vienna. It is now in Prague, in a sadly damaged condition.

Back in Nuremberg, Dürer began to receive further commissions for important altarpieces. In 1504 he painted "The Assumption of the Virgin" for Jacob Heller, showing the crowning of Mary in Heaven while below the apostles watch and pray by the shores of a lake. Unfortunately, this picture was destroyed by fire and only a copy remains. But the lovely drawing of the praying hands of one of the apostles (see p. 44), every vein and line perfectly portrayed, is in the Albertina Gallery in Vienna, with studies for the apostles' heads.

Dürer's most elaborate religious painting, and one which is still in a

DÜRER   *Pinakothek Gallery, Munich*

THE PAUMGARTNER ALTARPIECE

A curious composition, in which the main scene is the Nativity. The large figures of Joseph and Mary are surrounded by tiny doll-like representatives of the donor and his family, presumably to emphasize the importance of the main characters. The two Paumgartner brothers appear on the wing panels as St George and St Eustace.

DÜRER British Museum

HOUSE BY THE POND

good state of preservation, is "The Adoration of the Trinity", now in Vienna. It is splendid in colour and great skill is evident in the painting of the bishop's robes. But the most memorable part of the picture is the kneeling knight in armour with his plain, homely but interesting face.

Two years before his death, Dürer painted on his own initiative two panels each depicting a pair of apostles, which he offered to the City Council of Nuremberg as a memorial to himself. On one side are St Peter and St John and on the other St Paul and St Mark. The figure of St John is particularly calm and dignified. It is thought that the panels were intended to be part of a larger composition which was never painted owing to the Reformation, which put an end to church decoration for the time being.

Dürer was engaged on many other projects during his career. For the Emperor Maximilian, to whom he was appointed court painter in 1512, he designed woodcuts of a great triumphal arch and a triumphal car. He illustrated the Emperor's prayer book with fascinating coloured drawings containing all manner of strange and exotic animals and birds. He also found time to write books on various technical subjects, such as geometry and perspective. He was known and respected by men of culture in many parts of Europe including the great Dutch scholar, Erasmus, whose portrait he painted, and he is said to have exchanged drawings with Raphael.

Dürer holds a unique position in German art which had hardly existed before his time, apart from the rather sweet and sentimental pictures of Stefan Lochner. His contemporaries were Grunewald, whose chief work was the grim Isenheim altarpiece, and Altdorfer, mainly a landscape painter. The only serious rival to Dürer was Hans Holbein a generation later, but his chief concern was with portrait painting. In the variety of his interests and achievements, Dürer can perhaps best be compared to Leonardo da Vinci. After his death in 1528, Martin Luther referred to him as "the best of men". He was certainly among the best of artists.

PRAYING HANDS
Albertina

7

Struggle and Splendour

MICHELANGELO

The Buonarroti family lived in the little town of Caprese near Florence, where Ludovico Buonarroti was Mayor. In 1475 his son Michelangelo was born there, a child destined to become the greatest painter, sculptor and architect the world has ever seen.

Michelangelo's mother died when he was very young and he spent much of his childhood at Settignano among the stone cutters who quarried and hewed the white marble. There he first learned to love the stone which he later carved with such wonderful skill.

When the family moved to Florence, he was apprenticed, much against his father's will, to a well-known painter Domenico Ghirlandaio, whom he helped with some frescoes in the church of Santa Maria Novella. But his whole passion was for sculpture and in 1489, he became the pupil of Bertoldo, who had a school for young sculptors in the gardens of the Medici Palace. There he was noticed by Lorenzo the Magnificent who was so impressed by the boy's work that he invited him to live in his own palace, where he met Lorenzo's circle of friends, poets, scholars and artists who called themselves "Humanists" and discussed every possible subject of interest to man. During this quiet happy period, Michelangelo produced his first religious sculpture "The Madonna of the Stairs".

After the early death of Lorenzo in 1492 everything was changed. He was succeeded by his son Piero, a weak and arrogant man who gave Michelangelo only one commission - to make a statue out of snow. Piero was quite unable to keep order in Florence. Savonarola was calling the people to repentance while a French army was getting ready to invade the city. The Medici were driven out and Michelangelo was forced to flee, first to Bologna, then to Venice.

In 1496 he went to Rome; two years later when he was only twenty-three, he carved his first great masterpiece, the beautiful "Pietà" now in St Peter's, in which he represents the Madonna as still a young and lovely woman, supporting the graceful, lifeless body of her son.

MICHELANGELO   *Uffizi Gallery, Florence*

THE HOLY FAMILY

After the death of Savonarola in 1498, Michelangelo was able to return to Florence. In 1501, he started to carve the huge statue of David, which is more than sixteen feet high. The original statue is now in the Accademia Gallery; a life-size copy stands in front of the Palazzo Vecchio. Another commission of about this time was the "Madonna and Child" for Bruges Cathedral. Here was foreshadowed Michelangelo's briliance in making his figures live; the child seems to be clutching his mother's hand as a protection from something which frightens him. This feeling of life and movement is even more intense in the unfinished "Madonna and Child" which is now owned by London's Royal Aca-

MICHELANGELO   *Sistine Chapel, Vatican*

THE LIBYAN SIBYL

demy. This child is positively shrinking away in fear from a goldfinch which is being offered him by the little St John, just as a real baby might do. In April 1965 it was decided to lend this picture to other countries as an "Ambassador of Peace".

While in Florence, Michelangelo painted one of his very few easel pictures. (See page 46) This is the "Holy Family", now in the Uffizi Gallery, a round picture or "tondo". The Madonna and St Joseph are struggling to prevent the child from leaping out of their arms. Nothing so arresting and lifelike had ever been seen before in Italian art. Two other paintings, "The Entombment" and "The Madonna and Child" in the National Gallery, are thought to be by Michelangelo and these three are the only pictures, apart from frescoes, that he painted. Unfortunately, Michelangelo never completed the "Battle of Cascina" which he was commissioned to paint for the Council Hall of Florence; it can be seen, however from copies of the preparatory cartoon, which shows soldiers surprised when bathing, how skilful he had already become in representing the human body.

It was about this time that Michelangelo first became involved in what was to prove the most difficult and frustrating undertaking of his whole life. He was asked in 1505 by Pope Julius 11 to design his tomb. It was to be an elaborate monument with forty statues, to be completed in five years and Michelangelo was to be paid ten thousand ducats when his work was finished. He was given only a thousands ducats to begin with, barely enough to pay for the marble. Actually he worked on it on and off for forty years and in the end only three statues by him, including the famous "Moses", can be seen on the monument in the church of San Pietro in Vincoli. No wonder one writer referred to the project as "the tragedy of the tomb" and Michelangelo himself exclaimed bitterly, "I have wasted all my youth chained to this tomb".

The project seemed to be under an unlucky star from the beginning. Michelangelo opened a workshop in Rome; he went himself to the quarries to choose the marble, but storm and floods hindered the delivery of the material. There were many other difficulties in the way. The Pope was domineering and Michelangelo having a sensitive nature, they often quarrelled. Michelangelo wrote in a letter that it would soon be a question not of the Pope's tomb but of his own. On another occasion, he observed that he wished he had hired himself out to make sulphur matches.

Julius died in 1513 and in all Michelangelo made five contracts for the tomb with different Popes. He was never able to devote himself wholly to the work because he was continually being given commissions for other big undertakings.

As early as 1508, when he was only thirty-three and busy on designs for the tomb, Pope Julius decided that the ceiling in the Sistine Chapel in the Vatican, which was then designed as a blue vault with gold stars, should be painted with frescoes and he summoned Michelangelo to undertake the work. In vain the artist pleaded that he was a sculptor and not a painter. The Pope was adamant. He was a powerful patron and Michelangelo wanted to earn money to help his father and brothers, who made continual demands on his generosity. So at last he agreed and produced one of the most amazing works of genius in the world.

The walls had already been decorated with beautiful frescoes by Botticelli, Perugino and other well-known artists. In order to paint the ceiling, Michelangelo had to lie flat on his back strapped to a platform. He did all the actual painting himself, using assistants only to fetch and carry for him. The technique of fresco painting is to cover the surface first with a lime wash on which the painting has to be done while it is still damp. A preliminary cartoon or drawing is stuck to the surface, outlined by an iron stylus, then removed and the outline painted over but not necessarily followed exactly. Only a certain amount of work can be done each day, as the plaster must not be allowed to dry. When the work is finished, it is then left for six weeks before being sized over. Beautiful pastel effects of colour can be obtained in fresco painting, but there are fewer varieties than in easel painting and dramatic effects of light and shade are not possible.

The central theme of the frescoes, which took four years to complete, is the creation of the world and of man, and the origin of sin. The best known of the nine scenes is that in which God holds out his hand to meet the hand of Adam whom He has just created. At the corner of each picture are seated lifelike figures of young men, the "Ignudi", bearing garlands. Above, below and at each end of the central pictures, Michelangelo created the figures of prophets and wise women, painted to look like statues carved from marble. Words cannot describe the nobility of their faces, Jonah and Daniel young and vigorous; Isaiah and Joel strong and thoughtful; Jeremiah in deep meditation. The four triangles at the corners of the ceiling are filled with paintings of men and women from the Old Testament triumphing over evil, Moses and the brazen serpent, Esther and Ahrasuerus, Judith and Holofernes.

Other spaces contain pictures of the ancestors of Christ, Jacob and Joseph, David and Solomon.

In his paintings, Michelangelo uses the human figure as almost his only means of decoration. When he was young, he spent much time dissecting bodies to see how they worked, and he makes use of this wonderful knowledge in the figures he created. Landscapes, flowers and animals, colour arrangements play a much less important part in his composition.

The Sistine Chapel was finished in 1512 and Michelangelo then continued work on Pope Julius' tomb until 1516, when he returned to Florence where the Medici were temporarily in control again, this time to work as an architect on the façade of the Church of San Lorenzo which the new Pope Leo X commissioned. The contract was signed and a model made, but owing to disagreements the work was never done and the front of the church remains rough and unfinished to this day.

YOUTH
Sistine Chapel

MICHELANGELO   *Medici Chapel, Florence*

Statue of LORENZO DE MEDICI
(Duke of Urbino)

Perhaps the most perfect work of architecture and sculpture designed by Michelangelo was the Medici Chapel in Florence, which he started in 1520. It was intended as a memorial to four members of the Medici family, Lorenzo the Magnificent, his brother Guiliano, his son, another Guiliano, the Duke of Nemours, and his grandson Lorenzo, Duke of Urbino. Eventually only the tombs of the two dukes were placed there, with statues carved by Michelangelo in niches above. These were not true likenesses of the dukes for, as Michelangelo said, in a thousand years' time nobody would know or care what they looked like. Lorenzo is supposed to typify the studious and Guiliano the active life. Beneath each statue are two splended carved figures symbolizing the times of the day, Dawn and Evening beneath Lorenzo, and Night and Day under the statue of Guiliano. The two male figures are unfinished and so is the beautiful Madonna and Child on the end wall, one of Michelangelo's most lovely and spiritual creations.

The work in the chapel was not finished until 1534 owing to the invasion of Italy by foreign troops and the expulsion again of the Medici from Florence. During this time Michelangelo was employed as a military engineer. In spite of his debt to Lorenzo the Magnificent, his sympathies were with the Republicans. He helped to fortify Florence against the Medici and was branded by some as a traitor.

The last work in the chapel was done by assistants and in 1534 Michelangelo left Florence to spend his remaining years in Rome. About this time his father died and he met Vittoria Colonna, who was to be his great friend until her death in 1547.

He hoped now to be left in peace to finish the tomb of Julius, but a new Pope Paul III had appeared on the scene and he decided that Michelangelo should paint a new fresco on the end wall of the Sistine Chapel, above the high altar. Paintings which were already there had to be removed to make room for it. The theme of the picture was "The Last Judgement". It takes up nearly two thousand square feet and is the largest fresco in Rome. It took Michelangelo five years to complete it. He painted the whole picture himself mounted on scaffolding, from which he once fell and hurt his leg. He was probably faint from lack of food, for it is related that when he was engaged on his great works he lived for days on a crust of bread and snatched a few hours' sleep in his clothes. He was completely dedicated to his art.

The central point of the picture is the figure of Christ, not a gentle, bearded saviour but a young, vigorous figure with arm upraised. The Virgin is beside him and around are hosts of apostles, martyrs, prophets and holy women; their bodies tense, their faces turned eagerly to Christ. Above angels hold the symbols of the Passion, the cross and the column at which Christ was scourged. In the middle zone are people who have been judged, on the left the righteous, on the other side the wicked condemned to Hell. Between the two groups are angels blowing trumpets. The lowest part shows the resurrection of the dead and the damned being ferried over the river Styx by Charon, the dark boatman.

This great and terrible picture dominates the Sistine Chapel although it has been much tampered with since it was painted. Goethe, the great German poet, remarked, "No one who has not seen the Sistine Chapel can have a clear idea of what a human being can achieve".

Michelangelo was sixty-six years old when the "Last Judgement" was finished in 1541, but much remained to be done. He painted two more frescoes "The Conversion of St Paul" and "The Crucifixion of St. Peter" for Pope Paul 111's chapel in the Vatican. When he was well over seventy, he carved a Pietà intended for his own tomb in which he included his self-portrait in the guise of the old Nicodemus. He somehow managed to break the sculpture, either accidentally because the marble was hard or on purpose because his own work did not satisfy him. It is now in Florence Cathedral.

Many great architects, including Raphael, helped in the building of the new church of St Peter's. In 1547 Michelangelo, at the age of seventy-two, was put in charge of the building work. His actual share was to be the construction of the dome, for which he made a model, but he only built the drum or inside part.

And so this great old man went on working until he was nearly ninety. Early in 1564 he caught a chill, but he would not rest and went wandering about in the rain. On February 18th he died, leaving his last sculpture, the deeply moving "Rondanini Pietà", unfinished.

Michelangelo's work shows to what pinnacles of greatness a man can attain. In addition to his achievements as sculptor, painter and architect, he was a poet and wrote some sonnets. His personal life was not a happy one. His father and brothers were a continual source of worry, with their constant demands on him. He was sensitive about his appearance (his nose had been broken in a fight when quite young.) He had little time for social life and made few friends, because he imagined people despised him. He disliked Raphael for this reason, although the younger artist sincerely admired and learnt much from him. He experienced many frustrations in his work, both because he was obliged to undertake what his patrons wanted, and also because at times his hands could not keep pace with the grandeur of his ideas. Nevertheless, out of his struggles and frustrations came the greatest and noblest works of art that the hand of man has ever been able to create.

8

Twenty Crowded Years

RAPHAEL

The sun must surely have been shining on the green hills of Umbria in Northern Italy when Raffaello Sanzio (known as Raphael) was born in 1483 in the town of Urbino. This boy seemed to be endowed with all the gifts of the gods, growing up to be handsome, popular and extremely talented. His father was a painter, so his entrance into the world of art was easy. The churches and splendid ducal palace of Urbino were full of paintings by great masters and he would also have gained inspiration from the lovely tranquil countryside.

By 1500, Raphael was helping the well-known artist Pietro Perugino to decorate the Assembly of Hall the Bankers' Guild in Perugia. The boy learnt much from Perugino whose altarpieces with sweet-faced saints and lovely landscape backgrounds were already well known. Raphael's early work shows Perugino's influence. When he was about nineteen, he painted the beautiful little "Vision of a Knight" now in the National Gallery, in which a young knight in armour lies asleep dreaming of the two attractive women, Duty and Pleasure, between whom he has to choose. This picture is exquisite in colour; behind the figures lie green fields stretching back to the river and the blue hills in the distance.

The most ambitious picture of Raphael's early period is the "Sposalizio" or "Marriage of the Virgin" painted in 1504 and now in the Brera Gallery, Milan, which shows the High Priest marrying Joseph and Mary, while an unsuccessful suitor breaks a rod across his knee as a sign of defeat. The faces are beautiful, but rather vague in the manner of Perugino. Here for the first time Raphael shows his interest in architecture. A temple designed by his friend Bramante, the foremost Italian architect of the time, fills the background. The picture is very lovely in colour. Another fine altarpiece of a rather formal kind, is the picture commissioned by the Ansidei family "The Ansidei Madonna" (National Gallery) which shows the Virgin and Child on a massive wooden throne with St John the Bapist and the dignified St Nicholas in bishop's robes standing by.

In the autumn of 1504, Raphael found his way to Florence, the centre of the great upsurge of interest in everything concerning the intellectual and artistic life of man which was called the Renaissance. There he studied the work of Leonardo da Vinci and another Monk of San Marco, Fra Bartolommeo, who was painting altarpieces in the same monastery where Fra Angelico had lived fifty years before.

The year 1505 was for Raphael the "Year of the Madonnas", for he painted many of his most famous at that time. Some of them show Mary seated with the Christ child and the little John the Bapist at her knees and a sunny country landscape behind. The Madonna is fair, serene and beautiful as she watches the little boys at play. Three of the best known of these Madonna pictures are "The Madonna in the Meadow", in Vienna (p. 57), "The Madonna of the Goldfinch" in the Pitti Palace and the lovely picture in the Louvre known as "La Belle Jardinière" ("The Beautiful Gardener") in which the landscape is particularly gay and beautiful.

A Madonna of a different kind, but no less exquisite, is the "Granduca Madonna", so called because it belonged to the Grand Duke of Tuscany who refused to be parted from it and carried it with him on all his travels. This picture is painted against a dark background, with no landscape; the Virgin holds the Child in her arms. Although the technique of oil painting had not reached Florence at the time of Raphael, he attains a delicately soft effect in the painting of the Virgin's face and hands and the plump little body of the baby.

Towards the end of his stay in Florence, Raphael attempted a really great subject in "The Deposition of Christ" which was commissioned for a church in Perugia by a lady who had lost her only son in a family vendetta. It is now in the Borghese Gallery in Rome. The composition and the colour of this picture are rèmarkable, but Raphael was not really able to portray the deep feeling of such a scene and the figures have an air of unreality.

In 1508 Raphael like many other artists went to Rome where Michaelangelo had just started to paint the ceiling of the Sistine Chapel. Pope Julius 11, a great patron of the arts, on whose tomb Michelangelo spent many distressing years, wanted his apartments in the Vatican, called the Stanze, decorated with wall paintings and the task was entrusted to Raphael. The most important stanza (room) was "The Stanza dell' Segnatura" where important documents were signed and Raphael started his work there, choosing for his theme man's struggle to attain perfection in religion, philosophy and the arts. The first fresco was called "La Disputa". This depicts, not a quarrel but a discussion between the Church in heaven with the Holy Trinity, the Virgin and St John the Baptist in the centre and the Church on earth, bishops, cardinals and scholars, grouped around the Holy Eucharist. Raphael had now begun to show his mastery of space composition. Here and in the other frescoes he grouped his figures in a most skilful way to fit the semi circular shape of the wall.

The most attractive part of the "Disputa" is the bottom left hand corner in which a handsome fair young man stands in front of a fascinating landscape in which, if it is studied in detail, men can be seen standing on scaffolding building a church. This is one of the graceful touches which add charm to many of Raphael's pictures.

The most important picture in the Stanza dell' Segnatura is "The School of Athens" representing "Philosophy". Famous Greek thinkers like Plato, Aristotle and many others are grouped together in a magnificent hall. Here Raphael was able to give full rein to his love of architecture in the painting of the arches, the columns and the flight of steps. He introduced portraits of his friends into the picture as was the custom at that time; for instance Bramante is shown as Euclid, Plato bears a strong resemblance to the now elderly Leonardo da Vinci and Raphael has included himself in one of the groups. There is one more noted fresco in the stanza, the "Parnassus", illustrating the arts, in which famous poets like Homer, Virgil and Dante surround Apollo, the God of Music, and the Nine Muses.

The Pope was delighted with the decoration of the Stanza dell' Segnature and in 1512, Raphael began the frescoes in the second room, the Stanza dell' Eliodor in which the theme was the intervention of God in human affairs. The main work, from which the room takes its title, is "The Expulsion of Heliodorus from the Temple". It illustrates a story from the Book of Maccabees in the Apocrypha in which Heliodorus tries to steal the treasure from the temple and is driven out by an angel in armour riding on a white horse. Pope Julius himself is shown looking on at the scene. The painting of the temple is magnificent, but Raphael rarely succeeds when he is trying to portray violent movement. More satisfying and beautiful in colour with its soft reds and blues, is "The Mass of Bolsena" in which the priest sees blood flowing from the chalice when he is celebrating mass in the church of St Christina at Bolsena. The Pope is kneeling with his Swiss Guards near the altar.

RAPHAEL   *Kunsthistorisches Museum, Vienna*

THE MADONNA IN THE MEADOW

"The Liberation of St Peter" has several interesting features. It is divided into three parts; on the left the guards are seen stationed outside the cell while the crescent moon shines outside the window; in the centre is the dazzling figure of the angel arousing St Peter, whom he leads to safety in the scene on the right. Night scenes like this are uncommon in Italian painting at this time and Raphael's skill in contrasting darkness and brilliant light is remarkable.

By the time Raphael started the frescoes in the third stanza, Pope Julius II was dead and his successor was Leo X, the son of the great Medici ruler, Lorenzo the Magnificent. The Stanza dell' Incendio contains one of Raphael's most ambitious works, "The Fire in the Borgo".

Before this third room was finished, Raphael was dead and the work was finished by his pupils and assistants.

It is necessary to go to Rome in order to admire the frescoes in the stanze but examples of Raphael's style at this time can be found in England. Pope Leo X wanted some tapestries to hang in the Sistine Chapel and he asked Raphael to prepare the preliminary designs or cartoons for these, each illustrating a scene from the New Testament. Seven of these cartoons are now in the Victoria and Albert Museum and they are large and impressive pictures in colour, although, of course, more roughly painted than finished work. Two of the best are the "Miraculous Draught of Fishes" (under) and "Feed my Sheep".

During the twelve years he spent in Rome, Raphael fulfilled an incredible number of commissions. Among them was the lovely classical fresco of "The Triumph of Galatea" in which the maiden in her flowing veil is seen driving a car drawn by dolphins while Cupids shoot their arrows from above. This was painted for the Villa Farnesina in 1514.

The Madonnas he painted in Rome are quite different from the fair Madonnas of the Florentine period. In the "Madonna of the Chair" (Pitti Palace), the young and beautiful, but rather worldly, mother clasps the child tightly in her arms. Of incomparable beauty and known in reproduction throughout the world is the "Sistine Madonna" which was painted in 1514 for the monks of San Sisto, Piacenza, now in the Dresden Gallery.

Some of Raphael's best portraits were produced during his last years in Rome, among them "La Donna Velata" (The Veiled Lady), and the fine portrait in the Louvre of his friend Baldassare Castiglione. Cardinals and Popes were among his sitters.

On the death of the great architect, Bramante, in 1514, Raphael was appointed chief architect in charge of the building of St. Peter's. He produced a plan for the new church, designed on formal, classical lines but it was never used. He helped in the building of the Vatican and also had a part in designing important buildings in Rome like the Villa Madama and the Farnese Palace.

In 1520, Raphael caught a chill and a week later he died, probably worn out with work, at the tragically early age of thirty-seven. He was buried in the Pantheon, the Roman temple which became a Christian church, where his tomb can still be seen.

What would Raphael have achieved had he been granted the life span of Michelangelo or even of Leonardo? This is a fascinating question but it is possible that he had already attained his full powers. In one or two of his late religious pictures, there is evidence that he might have developed the style called "Mannerism", the characteristics of which were over-sweetness and a rather theatrical exaggeration. As it was, he was one of the three greatest artists of the High Renaissance showing in his work, not perhaps the poetry of Botticelli, the enquiring mind of Leonardo, or the great strength of Michelangelo, but the interest in Greek and Roman culture which was so much in evidence at this time.

He had more influence on others than any of the great masters; Titian, Rubens, El Greco and many more owed much to their study of the famous pictures of Raphael.

TITIAN   *Kunsthistorisches Museum, Vienna*

THE GIPSY MADONNA

Notice the soft lines, and the natural background

9

The Great Venetian

TITIAN

In the Middle Ages Italy was a country of separate city states, each with its own ruler. The republic of Venice in the north, by reason of its position as a port on the Adriatic coast, was one of the richest of these. It traded with the East in silks and spices and had its own industries, in particular glass-making. Its rulers or doges lived in splendid style and so did its wealthy merchants.

Venice escaped many of the wars which ravaged other parts of Italy; the people enjoyed the pageants and processions which took place on saints' days in the squares and along the canals, in which the doges and senators took part, dressed in splendid costumes. Life was indeed pleasant in this city, where the sun shone on the sparkling water.

Early Venetian painting was very much in the Eastern or Byzantine style, decorative and brilliant in colour but flat and monotonous, without life or movement. Mosaic work was used in the decoration of St Marco and other important churches.

In the fifteenth century celebrated artists from other parts of Italy came to Venice to paint pictures in the new churches and public buildings. A visitor came in 1475 whose arrival was of great importance in the history of Venetian art. This was Antonello da Messina who is thought to have introduced the new technique of mixing paints with oil instead of egg, as in the older medium of tempera. Wood was the background of most tempera paintings, but oil paintings which now began to be done on canvas allowed of freer brushstrokes than the harder medium. Much softer and richer effects could be obtained, and much more variety in the blending of colours and contrast of tones, while outlines were less clearly defined.

The first great painter of the Venetian school was Giovanni Bellini, who was born about 1430 and died in 1516. He was the first Venetian artist to use the new oil technique. He broke new ground also in his use of landscape, not merely as a decorative background but as the scene in which his figures moved, an important part of the composition.

THE VENDRAMIN FAMILY ADORING THE TRUE CROSS

This is a formal picture evidently commissioned to celebrate some important event in the life of the family. Titian has succeeded magnificently in suggesting the texture of the rich crimson and purple fur-lined robes of the elders of the family and the bright red stockings of the smallest boy. Very beautiful too are the Cross and the Candlesticks on the altar. This is Venetian painting at its glorious best.

TITIAN   *National Gallery, London*

BACCHUS AND ARIADNE

TITIAN   *Borghese Gallery, Rome*

SACRED AND PROFANE LOVE

Like many famous artists, Bellini had a school, and his greatest pupil was Tiziano Vecelli, whom we know as Titian.

Titian was born in the little mountain village of Pieve, in the Alpine region of Cadore. The actual date of his birth is uncertain. He is known to have died in 1576, some people say at the age of ninety-nine, which would put his birth date at 1477, but he was probably born a few years later than this. He came to Venice when he was very young to be trained as a painter. Giovanni Bellini taught him his trade and he also learnt much from another artist, Giorgio Barberelli, known as Giorgione, an extremely gifted painter whose career was tragically cut short when he died of plague in 1510 at the age of thirty-five. Only one picture can be attributed to Giorgione with absolute certainty, the lovely serene "Madonna and Child with St Francis and St Liberale" in the cathedral of his home town of Castelfranco, a picture which seems to be surrounded with light and air. Giorgione's pictures are full of glowing colours and atmosphere; the figures are vague and mysterious as though living in a dream world of their own. It is fascinating to imagine how he would have developed had he lived; though he could hardly have rivalled Titian in greatness.

Titian's first commission was to help Giorgione to paint frescoes for the headquarters of the German merchants in Venice. All these have long since perished. In 1511 he went to Padua for two years to paint a series of pictures about the miracles of St Anthony of Padua.

The early style of Titian was much like that of Giorgione and it is sometimes difficult to disentangle the work of the two artists, especially as Giorgione is thought to have left several unfinished pictures which were completed by Titian. Among these is the "Noli me Tangere" ("Touch me Not") in the National Gallery in which Titian shows already his supreme skill in oil painting, using his favourite colours of red and blue.

There is something of mystery in every great artist, perhaps in Titian more than any other, not the vague other-worldliness of Giorgione but something deeper and more mystical, peculiar to himself. This element appears in his early portraits, particularly in the "Unknown Man" in the National Gallery, once thought to be a portrait of the famous writer Ariosto. There he is, dressed in a beautiful blue quilted garment, with his crafty, sinister, aristocratic face, looking as much alive as any spectator in the gallery. The picture is uncanny in its knowledge of character, one can almost imagine "Ariosto" coming out of his frame when the gallery is closed for the night, to engage in some nefarious activity.

All through his career Titian painted Madonnas. One of the earliest is the beautiful, dark-haired "The Gipsy Madonna" or "La Zingarella" (p. 60). At that time what were called "Sacred Conversation Pieces" were becoming fashionable in Venice. These were small pictures of the Madonna and child, with one or more other saints and often accompanied by the little St John. Sometimes St Joseph is there too and there are often animals. Titian painted several sacred conversations, "The Madonna with the Cherries", in Vienna, "The Madonna and Child with St Catherine" in the National Gallery, and "The Madonna with a Rabbit" in the Louvre, in which the soft lines of the Child's body and the beautiful Venerian features of St Catherine are exquisitely portrayed.

Among Titian's mythological and allegorical subjects is the charming "Three Ages of Man", which shows Giorgione's influence. Three babies, or "putti" as they are called in Italian, lie asleep, while a shepherdess pipes a love song to her sweetheart, and in the background an old man sits gazing at a skull. More important is a picture which raises many questions, "Sacred and Profane Love". (See page 63)

Titian loved to paint beautiful women, like "Flora" in the Uffizi Gallery with her splendid red-gold hair, the colour which was named after him, and "La Bella" in the Pitti Gallery, in her richly embroidered dress.

For Alfonso d'Este, Duke of Ferrara, he produced the magnificent "Bacchus and Ariadne", a picture full of life and movement with Bacchus leaping from his chariot drawn by two leopards to pursue the fleeing Ariadne as she rushes towards the sea. There is a delightful touch in the figure of the bright-eyed little fawn swaggering along beside the chariot. (See page 63)

Titian, although he has been accused of being hard, worldly and cold, delighted in the beauty of children and animals. In his "Flight into Egypt" (Prado, Madrid), there are rabbits, sheep and ducks around the Holy Family, while the donkey grazes contentedly in the background. One of the most delightful of his drawings is of a shaggy, rough-haired dog.

In 1516 Titian succeeded Giovanni Bellini as the official painter to the Republic of Venice. His first assignment was to paint a large altarpiece, "The Assumption of the Virgin", for the Frari Church. It depicts in a highly dramatic fashion the ascension of Mary into heaven surrounded by angels, while below the disciples wave farewell. It is painted in the rich glowing reds and blues which Titian loved, but the church authorities were at first reluctant to accept it, considering it too theatrical and worldly. In the same church there is another fine altarpiece by Titian, the "Madonna and Child" which he painted for the Pesaro family, with portraits of the donor and his family.

By 1525 Titian was firmly established as the foremost painter in Venice. He married in that year, but his wife Cecilia died in 1530, leaving him with two sons, Orazio, who helped in his studio, and the wastrel Pomponio, and a daughter Lavinia whom he painted several times. After his wife's death his sister Orsa kept house for him in his grand new home on the banks of one of the canals where he lived comfortably for the rest of his life.

Not only the rulers of Italy, but most of the crowned heads of Europe clamoured for his work. For Francesco Maria Della Rovere of Urbino he painted the "Venus of Urbino", one of his most famous pictures. He painted portaits of many influential people, two of the most notable being the young nobleman, Ippolito Riminaldi, who used to be known for some reason as the "Young Englishman" and Ippolito de Medici, grandson of Lorenzo the Magnificent, a dashing dark-eyed figure in a rich Hungarian costume of purple velvet. Both these pictures are in the Pitti Palace, Florence.

In 1533 the Emperor Charles V appointed Titian as his official portrait painter, because he was so pleased with his picture of him with his dog. Titian held this position for many years and in 1548 he went to Augsburg to paint what was perhaps his greatest portrait, "Charles V On Horseback". Philip II of Spain was another of his royal patrons; a portrait of him was sent to Queen Mary of England who was so impressed by it that she decided he should be her husband.

As a portrait painter Titian has perhaps no equal. It is true that he only painted important and aristocratic people; he would not have been interested in the court dwarfs and servants on whom Velázquez bestowed so much care, or the homely faces that Rembrandt loved. On the other hand, while Velázquez painted only what he saw and Rembrandt added something of his own sympathetic understanding, Titian painted what he did not see, with an almost uncanny insight into the personality behind the face, which the sitter might not have wished to reveal.

And so Titian continued on his brilliant career. He had two great friends, Jacopo Sansovino, the City Architect of Venice, and Pietro

TITIAN

Prado, Madrid

CHARLES V ON HORSEBACK

Aretino, who was a kind of sixteenth century agent with a finger in most of the intrigues that were always going on in Italy. His portrait appears most unsuitably among the blessed in Michelangelo's "Last Judgment". Titian made a splendid picture of this colourful character with his handsome, insolent face. It is said that Aretino while attending a banquet ate so much and laughed so heartily at some ribald joke that he choked himself to death.

As Titian grew older he became more and more skilled in the actual putting on of paint, using his fingers as well as his brush to press on the thick rich colours. There is no finer example of this skill than the portrait group of "The Vendramin Family Adoring the True Cross" painted in the 1540's, and now in the National Gallery. (See p. 62.)

Even in old age the artist's hand did not lose its cunning. New portraits, religious and mythological pictures continued to appear. Titian painted himself at the age of about eighty and the portrait reveals him as a handsome aristocratic old man. Almost his last portrait, and one of his best, is the enigmatic likeness painted in 1568 of another of his friends Jacopo Strada, a sculptor.

If some of the late religious works such as "The Crowning with Thorns" in Munich seem to be inspired by a disillusioned bitterness, there is one which gives the lie to anyone who would accuse Titian of being superficial and cold. This is the "Madonna and Child" in the National Gallery, painted when he was about ninety. It is a tender and beautiful picture of the Mother and Child in a simple and natural attitude, depicted in lovely pastel shades of pink and grey, the soft outlines almost fading away into a misty background.

In 1576 the artist was engaged on painting an "Entombment of Christ" when he was stricken by the plague and died of it, as did Giorgione sixty years before. His picture was finished by another painter.

The art of Titian had a great influence not only on Venetian painters like Tintoretto and Veronese who followed him, but on Rubens, Rembrandt, El Greco, Velázquez, Watteau, even on the French Impressionists of the nineteenth century. He is worthy to be ranked with the greatest in the Arts, such as Michelangelo, Beethoven and Shakespeare, and he was given more than the alloted span of life in which to develop his genius.

10

The Artist from the Island

EL GRECO

Domenikos Theotokopulos was born about 1541 on the island of Crete in the Greek seas. Nothing is known about his parents or his childhood, but he must surely have been interested in the art of the island, brilliantly coloured pictures and mosaics by artists from nearby Byzantium and the sacred ikons or religious paintings of the Greeks.

At that time Crete was a possession of Venice, and when he was about twenty-five, young Domenikos left his native land to study art in Venice under the great Titian, then almost at the end of his long and brilliant career. From the Italian master he learnt the technique of oil painting in rich and glorious colour, with softened outlines and spendid effects of light and atmosphere. He probably helped Titian with one of his last great religious pictures, "The Martyrdom of St Lawrence". He also studied the work of two other great Venetian decorators, Tintoretto and Veronese.

In 1570 he went on to Rome and made a study of the great paintings of Michelangelo and Raphael. He was much impressed by Michaelangelo's understanding of the human figure and by the classical beauty of Raphael's compositions. The influence of all these great masters can be seen in one of his first paintings of "The Cleansing of the Temple", a favourite subject of his. This version was painted while he was still in Italy, and in it he has paid tribute to his teachers by including portrait heads of Titian, Michaelangelo and Raphael at the bottom right hand corner of the work, together with the head of his great friend, Guilio Clovio, a painter of miniatures. He stayed in Rome until 1576, and while there is said to have met many interesting people, including Cervantes, the author of *Don Quixote*.

After his stay in Italy, Domenikos went to Spain where he worked for the rest of his life. He was nicknamed "El Greco" (The Greek), the name by which he has been known ever since. He arrived in Spain at the time of the great Catholic revival inspired by the Jesuits, the Society founded by Ignatius Loyola in 1533. In the spring of 1577 he came to

Toledo, a city built on the slopes of a bare rock surrounded by pine trees and olive groves, which must have reminded him of his native Crete. In its deep bed below, the River Tagus flowed. Here sword blades were fashioned and silks manufactured and here, too, was the headquarters of the Spanish Inquisition, the terrible secret court which ordered the execution of heretics in the square in front of the cathedral. When El Greco painted a view of the city, he pictured it with a lurid thundery sky, its towers and spires picked out by a flickering light and the river twisting and winding below. The city appears as a background in several of his paintings.

This was the atmosphere in which the strange genius of El Greco developed. His first important commission was to paint an altarpiece for the church of San Domingo el Antiguo. The centre panel, "The Assumption of the Virgin Mary", very strongly resembles Titian's famous version of the same subject for the Frari Church in Venice, but there is deeper feeling in El Greco's work. In the nativity scene, the artist may have used his wife, Jeronima de las Cuebas, and his baby son as models for the Virgin and Child. "The Resurrection" scene contains a fine portrait of Don Diego de Castillo, the deacon of the Cathedral, who commissioned the work. Most typical of El Greco are the large figures of the two Saint Johns in the lower part.

The artist's great brilliance and individuality become even more evident in his next important work called "El Espolio" and depicting the scene in which Christ's clothes are removed before the Crucifixion. It is a wonderful composition, crowded with figures milling around Christ in the centre. (See p. 76.)

This picture created a furore, although it was too novel to be admired by everyone, and El Greco was obliged to paint several more versions of the subject. The original one is still in Toledo Cathedral.

By now El Greco had developed an original technique of oil painting. His method was to prime his canvas with a coating of white paste mixed with oil resin which he then covered with a second coating in white and black. The brilliant colours of lemon yellow, blue, red and green were obtained by laying on transparent oil glazes. Often, in the highlights, spots of the white underpainting show through. From the Venetian painter, Tintoretto, El Greco borrowed the idea of making wax models of his figures which he suspended from the ceiling on strings. He was also supposed to have kept in his studio a small oil version of every subject he painted.

At this time, King Philip II, after a life of wars and intrigues, was leading the life of a religious recluse in Toledo. He had just built the great palace of the Escorial. The fame of the young painter from Crete reached his ears, and it was for him that El Greco painted a picture called "The Adoration of the Name of Jesus" or "The Dream of Philip II". In this ambitious and brilliant work, the composition is in two parts. Above are angels adoring the Jesuit symbol IHS and a cross suffused with light; below, on the left, are the King, the Pope and the Holy Roman Emperor kneeling in prayer, surrounded by their followers who are gazing upwards, and on the right the mouth of hell is portrayed in the shape of a sharp-toothed whale swallowing up the damned. Between the two parts is a lurid and thundery sky.

There is a small preliminary version of this picture in the National Gallery which shows the brilliance of the colours.

The King shortly after commissioned another picture for the the Escorial. The theme chosen for this was "The Martyrdom of St Maurice". Maurice was a Christian soldier serving under one of the Roman Emperors, who chose martyrdom when he refused to obey orders to persecute other Christians. El Greco shows St Maurice in the centre of the composition talking to his officers while in another scene behind he is watching his soldiers being beheaded one by one. Angels are looking on from a lurid sky.

King Philip did not like this picture at all and refused to accept it, so that any dreams El Greco might have had of being appointed court painter faded. However, nothing daunted, he went on to paint the masterpiece of his early period and perhaps of his whole career. This picture was commissioned as an altarpiece for the Church of San Tomé, where it still is. It is called "The Burial of Count Orgaz" and illustrates the legend that at the funeral of this fourteenth century nobleman, St Augustine and St Stephen came down from heaven to take part in the burial service. The composition is in two parts. (P. 77.)

This is a picture of very great nobility and beauty, rather subdued in colour but painted with great technical skill. It is one of the world's greatest treasures of art. Particularly noticeable are the grace and refinement with which El Greco has painted the hands: elegance of hands and feet is a characteristic of all his work.

This picture brought El Greco fame and fortune. He now lived in style in the Marquis de la Villena's palace in the rich Jewish quarter of Toledo. It was said that he even sent for musicians from Italy to entertain him and his guests at dinner. Requests for pictures were continually coming in, among them many commissions for portraits. El Greco was a fine portrait painter, although perhaps not possessing the insight of Titian, Rembrandt or Velázquez. He painted a memorable self-portrait about 1608, revealing a sensitive face with large dark eyes. His greatest portrait is the frightening picture of the Grand Inquisitor, Cardinal Don Ferdinando Nino de Guevara. The cold cruel eyes of this terrible man look out through his spectacles with penetrating shrewdness, as he sits in judgement in his chair of state, dressed in magnificent red robes.

Some of the religious pictures of El Greco's middle period, which he painted for various churches in and around Toledo, are works of great beauty and sweetness. Two of the most attractive are the Villa Nueva picture of the Annunciation with the lovely dark-haired Madonna and the angels all playing on musical instruments in a scene lit by flickering candlelight, and "St Martin and the Beggar" in which the handsome young saint in armour, riding on a beautiful white horse, stoops to cover the slim brown body of the beggar boy. This is one of the most elegant of all El Greco's compositions. It is in America now.

El Greco had certain favourite subjects which he painted over and over again in his career. They were nearly all taken from stories in the New Testament. The National Gallery has versions of the "Agony in the Garden" and "The Cleansing of the Temple": Both are typical of the artist's style in the brilliance of their colour schemes and the dramatic way in which the scenes are imagined. In "The Cleansing of the Temple" in particular many figures in violent movement are arranged with great skill.

As El Greco grew older, his religious feeling became more and more intense and his paintings began to take on an unreal and dreamlike appearance. One of the most extreme of these pictures is "the Pentecost" or "Descent of the Holy Ghost", in which the tension of the scene, illuminated by candlelight in contrast to the darkness, is almost unbearable. "The Opening of the Fifth Seal" painted about 1610 to illustrate an incident in "Revelation" is dominated by the enormous figure of St John with his outstretched arms. Perhaps the most famous work of this late period is "The Assumption of the Virgin" of about 1608, painted for the Church of San Vincente and now in the Museum at Toledo. Here the figure of the Virgin seems to span the distance between Heaven and Earth and to make them one. But the

onal Gallery of Art, Washington
dener Collection)

ARTIN AND THE BEGGAR

GRECO

Museo de San Vincente, Toledo

ASSUMPTION OF THE VIRGIN

EL GRECO

VIEW OF TOLEDO

loveliest thing in the picture is the painting of the angel's feet on tiptoe among the red and white flowers, a most exquisite and graceful touch.

El Greco died after becoming paralysed, in 1614. Like many of the other great artists, he left his last work "The Marriage of the Virgin" uncompleted. In mood, this painting resembles the last sculptured "Pietà" of Michelangelo.

Many of El Greco's masterpieces are still to be found in Toledo, the city in which he spent his life, but an astonishing number of his famous pictures are now in the United States.

Although he is thought of as the first great painter of Spain, El Greco did not found a school and he had few followers. His genius was unique; he succeeded in expressing the intense religious enthusiasm of his time; he also had enormous skill in producing elegant compositions and brilliant colour schemes. He is certainly one of the greatest religious painters of all time.

EL GRECO

The Metropolitan Museum of Art, New York
(bequest of Mrs. H. O. Havemeyer, 1929)

PORTRAIT OF CARDINAL DON FERNANDO NIÑO DE GUEVARA

EL GRECO   *Cathedral, Toledo*

EL ESPOLIO

Notice how this scene is full of animation, from the carpenter in the foreground putting the
nails on the cross, to the excited onlookers behind. Only Christ is calm and peaceful amid
the hullabaloo.

EL GRECO   *Church of San Tomé*

THE BURIAL OF COUNT ORGAZ

In the lower part, the body of Count Orgaz is being lowered into the grave by St Stephen
and St Augustine. A priest and a monk stand by in amazement; in the background are
mourners in contemporary dress—these are mainly portraits of people, including El Greco
himself. The small boy in the front who is pointing to draw attention to the scene is El
Greco's son, then about eight years old. Above Christ and the Virgin Mary, saints and angels,
wait to receive the soul of the dead count.

11

The Artist-Ambassador

RUBENS

At the end of the sixteenth century the two parts of the Netherlands or Low Countries were torn apart by religious wars. Holland in the North was Protestant, while Flanders which we now call Belgium was a Catholic country under the domination of Spain. Protestants there had a hard time of it and so Jan Rubens who was a Protestant had to flee to Germany where his second son was born on St Peter and St Paul's Day in 1577. After Jan's death his widow returned with her family to Antwerp where the children were brought up as Catholics.

Young Peter Paul, a good-looking and well-mannered boy, became a page in a noble family. This life, however, did not appeal to him and at the age of thirteen he made up his mind to be a painter. He worked under three masters and at the end of his apprenticeship he became a member of the Painters' Guild of St Luke.

At this time Antwerp, peaceful under its Spanish rulers, was becoming a centre for trade and commerce in northern Europe; in particular a market for the buying and selling of books and works of art. Buyers came from all parts of Europe to the annual fair, looking for pictures and sculptures.

In 1599 a new governor arrived in Flanders, Isabella, daughter of King Philip II of Spain, and young Rubens helped to design the decorations to celebrate her entry into Antwerp. The next year he set off to study in Italy where he copied pictures of the Italian masters in Venice, Rome and Genoa. He met the Duke of Mantua and painted several pictures for him. Even at this early stage of his career he made his entry into diplomatic circles and went to Spain with a gift of horses for King Philip III. He was obliged to return to Antwerp in 1608 as his mother was dying—unfortunately he arrived too late to see her.

Rubens now settled down to live and work in Antwerp. He became court painter to Isabella and Albert, her husband. There was plenty of work for an artist in the city. The new Catholic society of the Jesuits was building churches there and wanted decorations picturing the miracles of their founder Ignatius Loyola and others of their leaders. There were other prominent buildings to be decorated, official portraits to be painted and pictures supplied to foreign buyers.

Philip Rubens, the painter's brother, was town secretary at the time, and the handsome, accomplished Peter Paul was introduced to all the best people. In 1609 he married Isabella Brant, daughter of a prosperous lawyer, and built himself a fine house in the Italian style with a studio, galleries and courtyards which he decorated himself, and a large formal garden. Parts of this house can still be seen in Rubens Street.

So many orders were now pouring in that Rubens was obliged to start a factory in order to supply them; and for the next twenty-five years he sent pictures to all parts of Europe including England. People were clamouring to be his assistants and pupils. Van Dyck, who later came to England and painted portraits of King Charles I and all the important English families, was with him from 1618 to 1621.

The way Rubens operated was as follows: he would make the designs for the pictures and give them to his assistants to carry out. One assistant was employed to paint flowers, another animals, and so on. Then he would put the finishing touches to the work himself. His preliminary drawings and coloured sketches are often more attractive than the finished work. Of course his best pictures were entirely by the hand of Rubens, but it is important to remember that many which bear his name were not all his own work.

The output of his studio was incredible and Rubens' pictures are now to be seen in practically every gallery in Europe as well as private houses. Portraits, mythological and allegorical subjects, religious pictures and landscapes were all undertaken.

The first important pictures of the Antwerp period were "The Raising of the Cross" and "The Descent from the Cross" painted for Antwerp Cathedral. These reveal both the strength and weakness in Rubens' style. He did not show deep religious feeling (except perhaps in one or two works like his great Crucifixion scene, the "Coup de Lance"), and the treatment is inclined to be over-dramatic. But already his ability in composition and management of figures was evident, and so was his skill as a colourist. About this time appeared his first version of "The Adoration of the Magi" which he painted eight times. The best known of these pictures is in Antwerp, but an important version was bought for King's College, Cambridge, in 1961 for the sum of £275,000. (p. 84.) The kings are dressed in gorgeous robes and as usual

RUBENS   *Pinakothek Gallery, Munich*

RUBENS AND ISABELLA BRANT UNDER A ROSE-BOWER

with Rubens, one of them is a Negro. He often used his wife and children as models and his baby sons are in the delightful "Holy Family" in the Wallace Collection.

As a portrait painter Rubens, though successful in producing very fine likenesses of the important people he painted, seldom penetrated below the surface of his sitter's character.

Some of his best portraits are of his own family. Soon after his marriage he painted himself and his wife. This picture, "Rubens and Isabella Brant under a Rose-bower", is in Munich. (See p. 80.) Rubens painted many pictures of Isabella until her death in 1626. Their teenage sons, Albert and Nicholas, can be seen in a portrait of about 1625 in the Liechtenstein Gallery and there is a sketch in Vienna of Nicholas as a baby.

For twelve years or so life went on prosperously for Rubens. His workshop continued to produce religious pictures, boar and lion hunts, allegories and mythological scenes. There were wild battle scenes like "The Destruction of Sennacherib" and two "Last Judgements" containing huge numbers of figures.

The Dowager Queen of France, Marie de Medici, widow of Henri IV and mother of Louis XIII, heard of Rubens and in 1621 commissioned him to paint twenty-one large pictures of incidents from her life for the Luxembourg Palace. He went to Paris twice to work on this series, which is one of his most grandiose achievements. The pictures, which are brilliant in colour and splendid as decorations, are partly historical and partly allegorical; for instance in one of the most ambitious, the landing of Marie at Marseilles, her arrival is greeted by river gods and an angel playing a trumpet. The series now occupies a gallery in the Louvre.

About 1623 Rubens embarked on a diplomatic career. The Archduchess Isabella, with whom he was on friendly terms, wanted an alliance between Spain and England and Rubens was deputed to try to bring this about. He had already met the Duke of Buckingham, Charles I's chief adviser, in Paris. In 1628 he went to Spain on his political business, where he met the great Spanish painter, Velázquez. In 1629 he came to England. Charles I received him with great cordiality; he was knighted and made an M.A. of Cambridge University.

During the eight months he spent in England he painted a self-portrait, now at Windsor, and presented Charles with an elaborate allegorical picture called "Peace and War" which now hangs in the

National Gallery. Charles commissioned him to decorate the ceiling of the new banqueting hall in the Palace of Whitehall. These pictures were not sent to England until 1635 and owing to a mistake in measurement they did not fit properly Very little of the finished work was done by Rubens himself, but the paintings are typical examples of the half-historical, half-allegorical decorations in which he specialized.

Rubens' diplomatic missions were unsuccessful and he was often deceived by unscrupulous agents and politicians. He was glad to return to private life in 1633.

In 1630, at the age of fifty-three, he had married a girl of sixteen, Helen Fourment, daughter of a rich silk merchant. Like Isabella Brant, to whom she bore quite a marked resemblance, she made him a good wife and he painted her many times. It is interesting to note how much freer his technique has become, how much more rapid the brushstrokes, gayer the colour and less stiff the postures than in the portraits of his first wife. Particularly delightful are the portrait of Rubens and Helen with their small child in leading strings, and the brightly coloured sketch of Helen and her children in the Louvre. The brilliant National Gallery portrait, called the "Chapeau de Paille", is probably of Helen's sister, Susan Fourment.

During these last peaceful ten years of his life Rubens painted some of his best pictures, among them the "Kermesse", or "Country Fair", in the Louvre and the "Peasants' Dance" in Vienna, both full of movement and life. "The Judgement of Paris" in the National Gallery shows his great skill in flesh painting and the use of glorious colour.

Rubens was by now extremely rich and prosperous. In 1635 he bought a country house between Brussels and Malines called the Château de Steen, where he spent the last five years of his life. The Château appears in several pictures painted at this time. There is a fine one in the Prado, Madrid, called "The Morning Walk", which shows Rubens and Helen in their grandest clothes strolling in the gardens with a gorgeous peacock at their feet.

To modern eyes some of Rubens' most attractive pictures are his landscapes. The most important of these were painted late in his career, when he was at the height of his powers, particularly as a colourist. One of the most important and certainly one of the most attractive is called, "Autumn: The Château de Steen" in the National Gallery. It reflects the artist's sheer joy in putting on paint. The towered château is on the left among the trees, with the tiny figures

AUTUMN: THE CHÂTEAU DE STEEN

of Rubens and Helen standing outside and an angler fishing in the moat. In the foreground is a market cart with two horses; in it sits a woman dressed in a bright red blouse and blue skirt. A fowler hiding with his dog behind a fallen tree root chooses his target from among a group of ducks. Behind lies the whole fascinating panorama of the Flemish countryside—the stream with its rustic bridge, cattle grazing in the fields and light clouds fleeting across the sunny autumn sky. It is a masterpiece of contrasting tones and splendid colour.

Smaller but equally beautiful is the "Sunset Landscape" in which the golden scene is filled with light from the setting sun as the shepherd sits peacefully with his flock and his dog beside the stream. The Château appears in the right background. The "Rainbow Landscape" in the Wallace Collection shows the same countryside at harvest time with cattle grazing among the stubble under the wide arc of the rainbow.

Rubens suffered severely from gout in his last years. His last self-portrait of 1638 shows him as a sick man, no longer the debonair figure of earlier years. He went on working as far as he was able until his death in 1640, painting pictures for the King of Spain and other patrons.

Sir Peter Paul Rubens, unlike many artists, gained success and riches in his own lifetime. Handsome, prosperous, friend of kings and princes, he yet remained a modest, kindly family man. Among the enormous number of pictures for which he was responsible (about 600 in all) there was bound to be a proportion of second-rate work. However, no other painter has ever excelled him in the use of colour, and the world has been enriched by the splendid vitality and joy of living of the artist who loved to paint.

RUBENS   ADORATION OF THE MAGI   *King's College, Cambridge*

12

The King's Portrait Painter

VELÁZQUEZ

Everyone has heard of King Philip II of Spain who sent the Spanish Armada sailing up the English Channel in the days of Elizabeth I. His grandson Philip IV is not so famous, although there are probably more portraits of him than of any other king, for he was lucky enough to have as his court painter the famous Spanish artist Velázquez. Diego de Silva Velázquez was born in Seville in 1599, twenty years after the birth of Rubens. He was taught painting by an artist called Pacheco, whose daughter he married. He started his career by painting what are known as "genre" pictures, that is scenes of everyday life such as "An Old Woman Frying Eggs", "Peasants at Table" and so on. "Christ in the House of Martha and Mary", in the National Gallery, is a good example of this early style. A meal of fish and eggs is being prepared while Christ sits in a back room. "The Water Carrier of Seville", in the Wellington Museum, already shows Velázquez's skill in figure painting. These early works were very true to life, but were painted in sombre and rather unattractive shades of brown and green.

In 1623 while on a visit to Madrid Velázquez was asked to paint King Philip IV. The king was so pleased with the likeness that he invited the artist to become court painter and Velázquez lived at the court for the rest of his life.

Velázquez did not live the easy life of a courtier, however. His position involved a great deal of work which he conscientiously performed. He painted members of the Spanish royal family for almost thirty-five years and took immense trouble with his pictures, as the many alterations or "pentimente", which are revealed by x-rays of his works, show. He always tried to represent people as they really were, without flattery, but with sympathy and understanding.

An important event occurred in 1629. Rubens came to Spain on an important mission. He stayed for several months and spent a good deal of time with Velázquez. Noticing the sombreness of Velázquez's colour schemes, Rubens persuaded him to go to Italy to study the technique of the great masters. When he returned in 1631, his style had become noticeably freer and his colours richer.

The heir to the Spanish throne was Don Balthasar Carlos, who was born in 1629, and Velázquez painted this little prince many times. The first portrait shows him at the age of two with one of the court dwarfs and there is another, dated a year later, in the Wallace Collection. There is beautiful painting here in the stiff, formal dress, the pink sash and the silky golden hair of the delightful small prince.

About the same time Velázquez painted "Philip IV in Brown and Silver" a full-length portrait in rich costume of brown and silver. With typical sincerity the artist has portrayed the king's long pale melancholy face. These characteristics are even more marked in the head and shoulders portrait of twenty-five years later. Both are in the National Gallery. Perhaps the finest state portrait of Philip is of him in a magnificent costume of red and gold carrying a general's baton in the Frick Collection in New York.

Velázquez painted few religious pictures, but he shows sincere feeling in "Christ at the Column", in the National Gallery, and also in his beautiful "Crucifixion", both painted about 1631.

For the king's new palace of Buen Retiro, Velázquez supplied some fine portraits of the royal family on horseback. The king himself is there, also the queen, Isabella of Bourbon, in her magnificent state dress and young Balthasar Carlos, now aged about five, on his prancing steed. (See p. 89.) Perhaps the most dashing of all is the Count-Duke of Olivares, who presented the palace to the king.

For this palace Velázquez also painted, in 1634, the celebrated historical picture, "The Surrender of Breda", which commemorates the capture of the town of Breda from the Dutch in 1625. It shows the Dutch general, Justin of Nassau, handing over the keys of the city to the Spanish commander Spinola. It is a very fine composition, with the Dutch soldiers and horses on one side, the Spaniards on the other and the two leaders, both figures of great nobility, in the centre. In the background smoke rises from the burning city. The picture is sometimes called "Los Lanzas", from the rows of spears which are a prominent feature of the composition. It now hangs, like most of the king's paintings, in the Prado at Madrid. (See P. 92.)

Other fine pictures of this period were the series of portraits of the royal family in hunting dress which decorated the king's hunting lodge.

The king appears here with his brother Fernando and Prince Balthasar

VELÁZQUEZ   *Reproduced by courtesy of the Trustees National Gallery, London*

PHILIP IV IN BROWN AND SILVER

Carlos, posed against the fine scenery of the park. Velázquez enjoyed painting dogs, and there is a particularly fine hunting dog with Don Fernando. The National Gallery has a picture of a boar hunt in the park, painted in 1638.

Velázquez painted very few portraits of people not in any way connected with the court, but one must be mentioned, the "Lady with a Fan" (see p. 92), a portrait of a lady with large dark eyes who is thought to have been his own daughter Francisca.

At the court of Spain at that time there lived a large number of dwarfs, buffoons and jesters whose business it was to wait on and entertain the royal family. They had picturesque names like "The Child of Vallecas", "The Idiot of Coria" and "Don Juan of Austria". Velázquez painted many of them and the portraits of these poor, grotesque and often misshapen creatures are among his finest works. He even gave them a kind of nobility so that they do not repel, but inspire pity. They can all be seen in the Prado Gallery.

In 1649 Velázquez paid a second visit to Italy to buy pictures and other art treasures for the king's new palace of the Alcazar. His journey took him to Rome and while he was there he painted what must be considered one of the great portraits of the world. His sitter was Pope Innocent X, posed in his chair of state in rich red and white robes, holding in his hand a paper on which the artist has signed his name. With his usual frankness and almost uncanny understanding of character, Velázquez has succeeded in conveying the wily shrewdness of this hardheaded old prelate. The portrait is now in the Doria Gallery in Rome.

Another important picture Velázquez painted while he was in Italy found its way to England, and is now in the National Gallery. This is known as the "Rokeby Venus" because it once hung in Rokeby Castle. It shows a young woman lying on a couch looking into a mirror held by a chubby little Cupid. There is a beautiful softness in the flesh painting and in the rich red curtains and grey bed-cover.

On his return to Madrid Velázquez soon had to embark on another series of royal portraits. In 1649 the king married the young Princess Mariana of Austria who was related to him and had been intended as the bride of the ill-fated Prince Balthasar Carlos. Velázquez painted her in her stiff court dress with a tiny waist and huge skirt called a farthingale. In 1651 their daughter was born, the Princess or Infanta Margarita, of whom Velázquez made some charming portraits for her mother's family in Vienna, where they still are. The first one shows her at the age of two in an exquisite dress of peach and silver standing beside a table on which is a superbly painted vase of flowers. She is painted again at the age of five and at eight years old in a fabulous dress of blue and gold.

In 1657 a boy was born, Prince Philip Prosper, and in one of the saddest and most beautiful child portraits in history Velázquez painted this poor delicate little prince, doomed to die the next year at the age of three, with a little white dog looking as pathetic as his master.

Perhaps the most intriguing of all Velázquez' works was "Las Meninas" (The Maids of Honour) painted in 1656. The scene is the painter's studio where he stands, brush in hand, before a large easel. The composition of the picture is curious but it is probable that he is painting the king and queen who are out of the picture, standing where the spectator is when he looks at the painting, with only their reflection seen in a mirror. In the foreground stands the five year old Princess Margarita, preening herself in her party dress, with her maids of honour, Lady Mariana and Lady Isabella, beside her. A group at the side consists of two of the palace dwarfs and a large dog looking bored with the whole proceeding. Members of the palace staff are coming and going in the background. It is a little moment of history preserved for ever in paint. (See opposite.)

In 1659 Velázquez painted "The Tapestry Weavers". This is partly realistic and shows the workshop of the weavers, and partly mythological. There are many dogs in Velázquez' pictures, but this is the only one in which he painted a cat!

Early the following year he went to France with the king, who was taking his daughter Maria Teresa there for her marriage with Louis XIV. On the journey he caught a chill and three months later he died aged sixty-one.

Velázquez's life was a continuous story of hard work and faithful service to the king. He made little use of assistants and pupils, altering and improving his work himself until he was satisfied with it. By conscientious application he altered his style from the hard outlines and sombre colours of his early work to the flowing richness of "Las Meninas" and the late portraits. His brush has given immortality to the kings and princes, dwarfs and animals, of three hundred years ago.

VELÁZQUEZ   *Prado, Madrid*

DON BALTHASAR CARLOS ON HORSEBACK

VELÁZQUEZ   *Prado, Madrid*

LAS MENINAS

The Maids of Honour

This composition is skilfully managed, leading the eye from the figures in the foreground to
the light in the open doorway at which a man is standing. On the walls hang pictures by
Rubens. Note the gay little touches of red which brighten the dresses and the painting of the
little girl's silky golden hair in this superbly painted picture.

VELÁZQUEZ   *Prado, Madrid*

SURRENDER OF BREDA

VELÁZQUEZ

LADY WITH A FAN

Wallace Collection, London

13

Light and Shade in Amsterdam

REMBRANDT

Rembrandt van Rijn (Rembrandt of the Rhine) was born in 1603 in the Dutch city of Leyden where his father owned a mill near the banks of the river. His parents sent him at fourteen to the University of Leyden. But the boy had made up his mind to be a painter and eventually his father permitted him to study art, first in Leyden, then in Amsterdam under a painter called Peter Lastman. At the end of his training in 1626, he returned to start his career in Leyden.

In order to understand Rembrandt's work, it is necessary to know a little about his historical background. Holland had recently gained her independence from Spain, who still dominated the neighbouring country of Belgium. The sturdy, independent Dutch people had now begun to develop on their own lines, becoming a rich nation of traders and merchants and embracing the Protestant religion. Church decoration was not much encouraged and pictures were wanted chiefly for the houses of wealthy business men and for the halls of the civic guilds. Many talented Dutch painters made a good living in the seventeenth century by providing small intimate pictures and portraits, Vermeer of Delft and Jan Steen among them. In the painting of portraits Rembrandt's chief rival was Frans Hals, painter of the debonair "Laughing Cavalier".

Rembrandt's early works reveal his two chief interests and studies: people, and the effects of light on darkness. There are several pictures of elderly scholars, pinpointed by light while they are studying in dark rooms. One example, "The Philosopher", is in the National Gallery. He used his family as models for portraits—there are several of his mother; one in Wilton House, Dorset, shows the old lady reading, her glasses perched on the edge of her nose and there is a better known one, "Rembrandt's Mother Reading", in Amsterdam.

Throughout his life, he had a childlike delight in portraying people dressed up in fine clothes. The famous picture in Berlin called "The Man in the Gold Helmet" is a portrait of Rembrand'ts brother Adrian,

REMBRANDT   THE NIGHT WATCH   *Rijksmuseum, Amsterdam*

REMBRANDT   THE JEWISH BRIDE   *Rijksmuseum, Amsterdam*

painted much later in the 1650's. In some of his earlier religious pictures, Rembrandt rather overdoes the effect of splendid Eastern costumes, notably in "Belshazzar's Feast" of 1636, in the National Gallery, a rendering of the dramatic story from the Old Testament. However, the picture shows how skilful Rembrandt had become in the technique of applying thick layers of oil paint.

In 1631, Rembrandt left Leyden for Amsterdam where he lived for the rest of his life. There is no evidence that he ever left Holland, but he must have had the opportunity of seeing Italian pictures and engravings and was influenced by them.

He soon began to make his name as a portrait painter and in 1632 had his first important commission, a portrait group for the Amsterdam Surgeons' Guild. This picture, "The Anatomy Lesson of Dr Tulp", is a masterpiece in spite of its macabre subject, the dissection of the body of a newly executed criminal. The composition is an original one; the young surgeons to whom Dr Tulp is lecturing are grouped on one side and the body is placed in a perspective which makes it appear shorter than it is in reality. By portraying some of the young men as looking at the spectator rather then concentrating on the matter in hand, Rembrandt showed that he had not yet reached full maturity. The picture, smoothly painted, is almost a study in black and white, with the exception of a touch of lilac on one of the sleeves. (See p. 97.)

Many orders for portraits followed "The Anatomy Lesson"; not from aristocratic patrons but from ordinary citizens who were very like those of our own day and age, apart from the costumes; the old couple in the picture "The Shipbuilder and his Wife" in Buckingham Palace are always admired and so is the 83-year-old Françoise van Wasserhoven whose portrait showing her anxious wrinkled face under her white cap is in the National Gallery. Rembrandt always seemed to have a special sympathy with old people and a delight in painting them.

We know what Rembrandt looked like at every stage of his career, for he painted himself a hundred times, starting in 1627 when he was too poor to pay anyone else to model for him. He appears as an intelligent youth in the 1629 portrait at The Hague, and as a man who has prospered in the fine portrait in the National Gallery, painted in 1640.

In 1634, Rembrandt married his landlord's daughter, the gay and attractive Saskia van Uylenborch, who brought him a considerable dowry. With her he spent the happiest years of his life. A famous portrait in Dresden shows him with a glass in his hand and Saskia on his knee, looking as though he is thoroughly enjoying himself at a party. He painted his wife many times. The delightful "Saskia Laughing", also in Dresden, catches a fleeting moment of pleasure, and in a portrait at Cassel she is dressed in fine clothes and wears a red hat. Two portraits, one in the National Gallery, which is called "Saskia Van Uylenborch in Arcadian Costume", show her dressed to represent Flora, the Goddess of Flowers.

In 1640, Rembrandt bought a fine house in Amsterdam's Breedstraat and filled it with pictures and other treasures of art. He lavished extravagant presents on Saskia and lived altogether beyond his means. But his happiness was not to last long. After only ten years of married life Saskia died, leaving him with one son, Titus, their other three children having died as babies. There are several portraits of the fragile, golden-haired Titus; one shows him at his desk at the age of fourteen, and a very attractive one, "Titus Reading", now in Vienna, was painted three years later.

In 1642, the year of Saskia's death, Rembrandt produced the most famous picture of his career. Amsterdam at that time was very proud of her companies of militia and civic guards, and several artists were commissioned to paint them, including Frans Hals. Rembrandt was asked to portray Captain Banning Cocq's company of arquebusiers leaving their headquarters for a shooting competition. The result was the great picture known as "The Night Watch", so called because the strong contrast of light and darkness made people think it was a night scene; however, when it came to be cleaned, it was discovered that this was not so. "The Night Watch" is not merely a portrait group, but a dynamic and thrilling picture. As the Captain and other officers lead out the men with banners flying and a drum beating, the townsfolk gather to look on, a dog barks, a child runs forward to get a better view. The light falls full on the handsome captain in his splendid costume and glints on the rich red suit of another officer priming his arquebus. It is said that there were criticisms of the composition from some of the guards who were relegated to the darkness at the back of the picture, but at any rate, the work was accepted and Rembrandt was handsomely paid for it. It is now the great attraction at the Rijksmuseum, Amsterdam. (See p. 94.)

In his heyday, Rembrandt painted religious pictures and landscapes as well as portraits. The best religious works are very different from the pretentious "Balshazzar's Feast". The small "Christ at Emmaus" in the

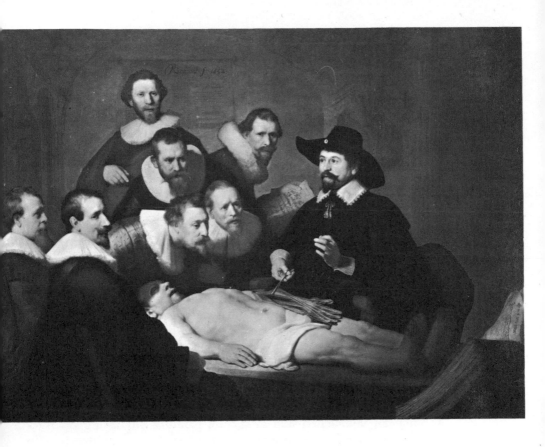

REMBRANDT

Mauritshuis, The Hague

THE ANATOMY LESSON OF DR TULP

Louvre (about 1640) is a simple, homely scene in which Christ, his figure bathed in light, sits with his disciples at a humble table, and in the very touching "Holy Family" in Leningrad, the young mother interrupts her reading to watch the child sleeping in his wicker cradle with its red coverlet, while chubby little angels keep watch above. "The Woman Taken in Adultery" of 1644 in the National Gallery, is an unusual and beautiful picture. As usual, the main figures are picked out by the light, the woman in her white dress, surrounded by her accusers, kneeling before the tall, kindly figure of Christ. In the dark background of the Church, the rich golden throne of the High Priest can dimly be seen. It is a picture with deep feeling, superbly painted. In his landscapes too, Rembrandt made play with sunshine and shadow, in such pictures of the Dutch countryside as the "Landscape with an Obelisk", "The Stone Bridge" and the appealing "Winter Landscape" at Cassel, with its stormy snow-clouds and bare trees.

During his prosperous years, many of Rembrandt's neighbours were Jewish merchants and traders, some of whom commissioned him to paint their portraits. He manages to record the eternal sadness of these Jewish faces, whether of Rabbi or merchant or an anonymous old man representing St Paul.

Probably the greatest of his single portraits is his study of his friend Jan Six, the Burgomaster of Amsterdam, painted in 1654. The handsome figure with his melancholy, sensitive face, appears against the usual dark background, wearing a black hat and holding his gloves, with his red cloak draped over one shoulder. Rembrandt had by now acquired an unmatched skill in texture painting and laying on thick layers of oils, a technique described by the Italian word "impasto". His colour arrangements are rich and splendid in contrast to the rather dull greens and browns of some of his early work. (See p. 103.)

After Saskia's death, Rembrandt was looked after by his housekeeper, Hendrickje Stoffels, of whom he became very fond although he never married her. We know her from several portraits, the best perhaps being the one in the Louvre in which she wears a pearl pendant and earrings. She looks less vivacious than Saskia, but has an honest, kindly face. She modelled for the lovely nude "Bathsheba", also in the Louvre, and for "A Woman Bathing in the Stream" in the National Gallery, a picture which repays careful study in order to discover the subtle richness of the technique as the woman in her white shift paddles her feet in the cool water. It is thought that the attractive "Girl at a Window" in the

REMBRANDT   TOBIAS AND ANNA   *M. van der Vorm Museum, Rotterdam*

REMBRANDT   THE THREE TREES   *Etching*

Dulwich Gallery may be a portrait of Hendrickje as a young girl.

Rembrandt's extravagance finally landed him in serious financial difficulties. He was declared bankrupt in 1656 and his house and all his treasured possessions had to be sold. His late portraits seem to mirror the disillusionment and suffering he must have endured at this time, for instance, the sad faces of the old couple Jacob and Margaretha Trip in the National Gallery, and in particular his last self-portraits. Gone is the assured, prosperous figure of twenty years before and in its place are the features of a suffering, broken man, old before his time. In the National Gallery portrait of about 1663, his features have coarsened and the face has a look of ineffable sadness. Portraits at Kenwood House and the Louvre, painted a year or two earlier, show the ageing Rembrandt at his easel. The last portrait, "Rembrandt Laughing" of 1668, with its senile grin, is almost unbearably painful but a masterpiece of broad, impressionistic brushstrokes.

Some important commissions came after Rembrandt's bankruptcy, one of them being the large show portrait "Man on Horseback" which the National Gallery purchased in 1959. His last great portrait group, "The Staalmeesters" or "Syndics of the Clothworkers' Guild", was painted in 1662. Rembrandt did not attempt to repeat the dramatic interpretation of "The Night Watch". This is a straightforward representation of six men at a table covered with a superbly painted red tablecloth. The picture makes an interesting comparison with "The Anatomy Lesson of Dr Tulp" painted thirty years earlier. In place of the eager faces of the young surgeons Rembrandt has portrayed world-weary elderly businessmen. The smooth painting of the earlier picture has given way to a much broader, more assured technique. The aged hand has certainly not lost its cunning.

THE SYNDICS OF THE CLOTHWORKERS' GUILD   *Rijksmuseum, Amsterdam*

During the last year of his life, Rembrandt painted two pictures of especial tenderness and beauty. The "Family Portrait" (at Brunswick) is a study of an unknown couple with their three small children. The mother's dress is the same rich red as the tablecloth in "The Syndics". The soft, blurred outlines of the figures seem to be merged into the dark background. The other picture, "The Jewish Bride" (in Amsterdam), is painted in the same mood of quiet tenderness, as the young couple in their splendid wedding clothes embrace each other. (P. 94.)

Rembrandt's last religious work, "The Return of the Prodigal Son", is a poignant version of the story as the old man emerges from darkness into light to embrace the penitent figure kneeling before him.

Hendrickje died in 1664, Titus his son in 1668 and Rembrandt himself died in 1669, a prematurely old and disappointed man, at the age of sixty-three. In addition to almost 600 pictures, he produced about 2,000 drawings and 200 etchings. Two of his best known etchings are the striking landscape "The Three Trees" (See p. 99), and the dramatic and moving "Christ Healing the Sick," called the "Hundred Guilder Print" because it is supposed to have once fetched that amount at an auction. It now belongs to the Rijksmuseum. Among his many realistic drawings of animals is a particularly lifelike and engaging "Elephant", in the British Museum.

Rembrandt, the greatest artist ever produced in Holland, deserves a place besides the great Italians, and Dürer, Rubens and Velázquez. His work can perhaps be compared with that of Velázquez, the great Spanish master. "The Night Watch" and "The Surrender of Breda" (Velázquez) though completely different in treatment and mood, are both masterly subject pictures. Both artists were splendid portrait painters but while Velázquez concentrated more on the very young, Rembrandt was interested in the old. He is the most human of all great artists and the characters he portrayed, Dr Tulp, Captain Banning Cocq, Saskia, Titus, Hendrickje, Jan Six, The Syndics and the artist himself, will live for as long as anyone looks at pictures.

REMBRANDT   *The Six Collection, Amsterdam*

PORTRAIT OF JAN SIX

14

Painter of the English Countryside

CONSTABLE

From the earliest times, landscape has played an important part in European art. Giotto and Fra Angelico in Italy, as well as Van Eyck and other Flemish painters, used natural scenery as a background for their religious pictures and later artists, particularly the Venetians, learnt how to set their scenes in a landscape rather than merely to use it as a decorative background. However, it was not until the seventeenth century that landscape painting really came into its own. Claude Lorrain, the French artist who worked in Rome, painted what were to all intents and purposes landscape pictures, although his romantic scenes always illustrated some biblical or mythological story. Some of Rubens' landscapes like "The Château de Steen" are among his best works. But it was in seventeenth-century Holland that such pictures first became popular, and the prosperous Dutch people bought them in large numbers to decorate their homes. Rembrandt painted several and artists like Ruysdael and Hobbema were well known for their view of the Dutch countryside. Hobbema's "The Avenue at Middleharnis" in the National Gallery is one of the most attractive.

In England, Gainsborough, the famous eighteenth-century artist, painted such landscapes as "The Watering Place" in the National Gallery for his own pleasure, although he earned his living by portrait painting. The classical landscapes of Richard Wilson were well-known and Turner began to produce beautiful watercolours at the end of the century. But the man who did most to put English landscape painting on the artistic map was John Constable.

Constable was born in 1776 in the village of East Bergholt in Suffolk. Like Rembrandt, he was the son of a miller, Golding Constable. He grew up near the places which have become famous in his pictures, the Stour Valley, Dedham Vale, Stoke-by-Nayland and Flatford Mill. He went to Dedham Grammar School and started to sketch and paint while he was still a schoolboy, under a sympathetic headmaster, Dr. Grimwood. After leaving school, he worked for a while in one of his father's mills, but his future was decided when he met Sir George Beaumont, an important art collector who used to come on visits to his mother at Dedham.

Sir George showed him one of his most treasured possessions, a small landscape by Claude Lorrain called "Hagar and the Angel" which he later bequeathed to the National Gallery. Constable was very interested in this picture, especially in the arrangement of trees, and copied it. About this time, too, he met the poet Wordsworth who loved Nature so much and said in one of his poems, "To me the meanest flower that blows can give, Thoughts that do often lie too deep for tears".

Through Sir George, Constable was persuaded to try his luck in London and in 1799 he finally gave up his work in the mill and entered the Royal Academy School, where he was able to study the work of other landscape painters. It was some time before he produced any important pictures of his own. He painted one or two altarpieces for country churches and earned money by executing commissions for portraits. He visited the Lake District in 1806 and saw watercolours by a gifted young artist called Girtin who died tragically young.

Constable's first picture for the Royal Academy called "The Stour Valley with Dedham in the Distance", though a little stiff and formal in arrangement, gave promise of what was to come. His first really important work was the "Dedham Vale" of 1811, a broad sweeping view of the countryside with the sunshine pouring down on to fields in the background and the foreground in shadow. This is reproduced on p. 107.

While he was still living at East Bergholt, Constable had met Maria Bicknell, the granddaughter of the rector of the local church. In 1811, they fell in love and wished to marry but owing to strong opposition, especially from her grandfather, they were not able to do so until 1816. In that year Constable painted her portrait which is now in the Tate Gallery. The marriage ceremony was performed by John's great friend, Archdeacon Fisher of Salisbury, with whom he often stayed and occupied his time by painting views of the Cathedral with its spire "darting up into the sky like a needle" as he expressed it. One of the most attractive views is the oil sketch in the National Gallery showing the river and the Archdeacon's house.

John and Maria spent their honeymoon at Weymouth and the unfinished "Weymouth Bay" in the National Gallery was painted at that time.

CONSTABLE   THE HAY WAIN   *National Gallery, London*

CONSTABLE   HADLEIGH CASTLE Oil study   *Tate Gallery, London*

CONSTABLE   SALISBURY CATHEDRAL FROM THE RIVER   *National Gallery, London*
Study   *Reproduced by courtesy of the Trustees*

CONSTABLE   DEDHAM VALE   *Collection of Major R. G. Proby*

After his marriage, Constable settled down to work in earnest and during the next twelve years or so produced some of his most important pictures, nearly all of them views of his native Suffolk. He was now able to build up satisfying compositions and his use of paint was becoming much bolder and freer. His methods were orthodox and he did not attempt anything startlingly original. His aim was to present the effects of cloud and sunlight on water, trees and fields. He had already produced "Boat Building" for the Royal Academy in 1815 and in 1817 came one of his most delightful compositions, "Flatford Mill", which shows a horse towing a barge along the banks of the Stour. In this picture there are reminiscences of "The Château de Steen" which he must have seen as it belonged at that time to Sir George Beaumont. Horses appear in a great number of Constable's pictures (he left some accomplished drawings of them too) and in 1819, the year he was made an Associate of the Royal Academy, he celebrated the honour by producing a large canvas called "The White Horse" in which the animal is standing in a barge. This is one of the few important Constables which have left the country; it was bought by Pierpoint Morgan the American millionaire.

In 1821, he painted what is generally considered his masterpiece, "The Hay Wain". Everyone knows this famous picture, with the farm cart ploughing through the water towards Willy Lott's cottage, in which its owner lived for nearly ninety years and which is a feature in several of Constable's paintings. But "The Hay Wain" is not merely an attractive landscape, a picture which is continually reproduced on postcards and calendars. It is a composition built up with immense skill and there is masterly handling of the effects of sunshine and shadow on the fields and on the water. Here, almost more than anywhere else, the artist expresses his love for this bit of Suffolk countryside that he knew so well. In 1824 "The Hay Wain" and another picture, "A View on the Stour", were shown at the Paris Salon and were awarded a gold medal. "The Hay Wain" made a great impression on French artists. Delacroix, an important French painter who was busy at that time on an elaborate Eastern scene called "The Massacre of Scio", decided to alter his work after studying Constable's technique. It is interesting to look at the oil study Constable made for "The Hay Wain", in the Victoria and Albert Museum, London.

Constable's married life continued to be happy. He lived first in Charlotte Street in central London, then in about 1820 he moved his

CONSTABLE

MARIA BICKNELL
(later Mrs John Constable)

CONSTABLE   *Tate Gallery, London*

ADMIRAL'S HOUSE AT HAMPSTEAD

wife and family to Hampstead. They lived in several different houses, finally settling in Well Walk about 1827. Constable used to walk to the top of Hampstead Heath to look at the clouds and the trees and to make sketches and studies of them. There is a beautiful painting of soft grey clouds in the Tate Gallery. One particular view over the Heath fascinated him and he painted it over and over again. It is from the West Heath looking towards Harrow, sometimes featuring the house called the Salt Box, sometimes Branch Hill Pond, both of which have now disappeared. "Admiral's House", which appears in a painting now in the Tate Gallery, is still there, although Crockett's Pond in front of it, from which a horse is drinking, has gone. So too have the village street, the cottages and the horse-drawn bus in the charming little picture called "A View of London with Sir Richard Steele's House" painted in the now dreary neighbourhood of Chalk Farm. The only familiar landmark is St Paul's in the distance. This picture, one of the most attractive small Constables, has gone to the Mellon Collection in the U.S.A.

All this time Constable continued to paint important pictures for public exhibition. In 1823, his subject was "Salisbury Cathedral", now in the Victoria and Albert Museum. He actually produced several versions of this scene, one of which has found its way to the Frick Collection in New York. In 1825 came "The Leaping Horse", a masterpiece which rivalled "The Hay Wain". Constable always took immense pains with these paintings, making preliminary sketches and often producing full size oil studies before making the final version. Some critics think that the study for "The Leaping Horse" is more vivid and lively than the picture itself. And, though lacking the final glazes, it gives an insight into the artist's technique of oil painting. Both the oil study and the picture itself can be seen in London; the former is in the Victoria and Albert Museum, the finished version belongs to the Royal Academy. One of the most appealing of Constable's pictures followed "The Leaping Horse". This was "The Cornfield", in which a small shepherd boy in a vivid red jersey lies flat on his stomach to drink from the stream while a dog drives the sheep along the lane and beyond is the sunlit field which gives the picture its name.

Constable's busy and full life in Hampstead was interrupted by the illness of his wife, who had never been strong. He used to take her to Brighton for her health (the large "Marine Parade and Chain Pier" in the National Gallery is a memento of one occasion) but she became gradually worse and died of consumption in 1829 when their seventh child was only a baby. In that same year, Constable was elected a full member of the Royal Academy. In spite of his great grief and depression, he continued with his work and in 1832 exhibited four oil paintings, including one which he had been preparing for fifteen years, commemorating the opening of the new Waterloo Bridge (not the one in existence to day).

Constable's later pictures are somewhat different both in mood and technique from those painted in the heyday of his career. The colours are darker and the paint is put on thickly with either a heavily loaded brush or a palette knife in non-transparent layers, a method known as scumbling, which gives a rough, broken effect. The mood of pictures like "Hadleigh Castle", for which there is a striking oil study in the Tate Gallery, and "The Cenotaph" showing a lonely stag standing in front of the memorial to Sir Joshua Reynolds, is sombre and gloomy. Even in "The Valley Farm" of 1835, in the Tate Gallery, although the scene is almost the same as that of "The Hay Wain" with Willy Lott's riverside cottage a prominent feature, the feeling of brightness and summer serenity seems to have vanished.

Constable had plenty to do until the end of his life. In 1830, he started to issue series of mezzotint engravings of his pictures, executed by a young man called David Lucas. In 1836, he lectured on landscape painting to the Hampstead Scientific and Literary Society. In his later years he suffered much from rheumatism and he died suddenly in 1837 at the age of sixty. He is buried in Hampstead Churchyard.

There is ample opportunity to study the work of Constable in London, in the National and Tate Galleries and in the Victoria and Albert Museum, to which his daughter gave many of his sketches, oil studies and some watercolours. See also reproductions on p. 106/7.

The inspiration for Constable's finest pictures came from one small part of the English countryside where he was born and spent his childhood. During the whole of his career of over thirty years he remembered and loved the barges and the wagons, the horses and sheep, the farms and cottages of the Stour Valley. He painted scenes with the sun shining on the fields or with clouds scudding across the sky, the trees rippling in the breeze and the shadows reflected in the water. He himself said, "I associate my careless boyhood with all that lies on the banks of the Stour. These scenes made me a painter and I am grateful". They helped to make him one of the most gifted landscape painters of all time.

15

Paris 1860-1880

MANET

There is no figure in French art to compare with the early great masters of other countries, Rembrandt, Rubens, Velázquez, Dürer. The best French painters of the seventeenth century, Nicolas Poussin and Claude Lorrain, spent practically all their working lives in Rome and their style is more Italian than French. Antoine Watteau, the brilliant painter of elegant out of door scenes called "Fêtes Galantes", who might have become a great master, died of consumption at an early age. The classical David and the romantic Delacroix, though important, are rather limited in their appeal. It is not until the nineteenth century that French painting began to develop in a way that led up to the work of the brilliant group called "French Impressionists". The man who did most to bridge the gap between the older more conventional methods and the revolutionary attitude to colour and light of the Impressionists was Edouard Manet.

Manet was born in Paris in 1832, the son of an important government official. When his father opposed his wish to become a painter, the impetuous young man ran off to sea and sailed to South America. On his return, his father relented and allowed him to study art. He travelled abroad to Germany, Italy, Austria and later Spain, and also spent many hours in the Louvre, copying pictures of the painters he most admired, Titian and Velázquez, Rembrandt and Frans Hals.

Manet's career did not have a very auspicious start. He was anxious to be represented in the Salon (the French "Royal Academy") but the first picture he offered to them in 1859, a realistic scene from low life called "The Absinthe Drinker", was rejected. However, two years later the attractive, rather more conventional, portrait of his parents was accepted. (See frontispiece.)

There was nothing of the struggling artist about Manet. A well-dressed handsome young man-about-town, he began to choose for his subjects portraits of well known people in the artistic and literary circles in which he moved, and scenes from life in the gay city of Paris, like "Music in the Tuileries Gardens" (National Gallery). In those days, the Emperor Napoleon III was often in residence in the Tuileries Palace and people used to stroll and sit in the gardens to listen to the band. Manet has pictured such a scene. (See p. 119.)

This picture was considered very modern and in it Manet revealed his new technique in which the composition was held together more by the colour then by drawing, indeed some of the faces are no more than sketched in, giving the picture an unfinished look. In a new kind of painting called "Peinture claire", the lighter colours were put on first, then the darks added before the lighter paint had time to dry; by this method, an effect of variety and movement was obtained, although a high degree of smooth finish was not possible.

Spain and Spanish art always appealed strongly to Manet and one of his most colourful early portraits is the one painted in 1862 of Lola de Valence, a Spanish dancer then appearing in Paris. Her full skirt is covered with rich patterning in green, blue and red.

Manet had no wish to be considered a rebel against authority and he went on offering pictures to the Salon. However, the work he submitted in 1863 "Déjeuner sur l'Herbe" caused a scandal. The picture was not intended to shock; it was indeed inspired by a picture by Giorgione "Fête Champêtre" and is a very accomplished piece of work. It was refused by the Salon but was afterwards shown at an exhibition called the "Salon des Refusés", consisting of works rejected by the Academy. Manet's picture of 1865 which the Salon did accept almost caused a riot when it was exhibited. This was the famous nude "Olympia", inspired by Titian's "Venus of Urbino". Manet was very upset at the reception given to the picture, which he considered his best and kept in his own studio until his death. The Salon authorities were now getting tired of the trouble Manet's pictures were causing and they turned down "The Piper", the portrait of a boy fife-player in the red and black uniform of the Imperial Guard. He was also forbidden to exhibit a controversial picture he painted in 1867 called "The Execution of the Emperor Maximilian". Maximilian was an unfortunate Austrian prince who was invited to become Emperor of Mexico, then under French rule. The French later withdrew from the country, leaving him to the mercy of the Republicans who captured and shot him at Queretano. In Manet's picture, which is now at Mannheim, the fatal volley has just been fired. The National Gallery has two fragments of another version of this picture, one of which shows the half dozen soldiers in the act of firing,

MANET   *Kunsthalle, Mannheim*

THE EXECUTION OF THE EMPEROR MAXIMILIAN

the other an officer attending to his rifle. Although the scene took place in Mexico, the soldiers are wearing French uniforms.

Manet painted a good many portraits of his family and friends, including several of his wife. They are usually what might be called "painterly" pictures with more attention given to the actual putting on of paint and the richness of surrounding details than to the character of the sitters. "Eva Gonzalez" in the National Gallery, a portrait of one of his pupils sitting at her easel in a white dress, painting a flower piece, is a typical example, so is the portrait of the famous writer Emile Zola, one of Manet's staunchest champions, seated in his study against a background of Japanese prints which were popular in Paris at the time. Manet was always fond of still life; he painted several superb pictures of flowers, peonies, tulips and roses in vases decorated in Japanese style.

In 1868, Manet was busy with a portrait group called "The Balcony", an interesting picture because one of the ladies depicted in it was Berthe Morisot, wife of his brother Eugène and one of the very few important women painters in European art. Her attractive picture, "Jour d'Eté" (Summer Day) is in the National Gallery.

Manet fought and helped to defend Paris in the Franco-Prussian War of 1870. At the end of the war, he was so exhausted that he was obliged to recuperate in the south of France. There he painted "The Port of Bordeaux" a fine sea picture showing the harbour crowded with fishing boats. The pastel pink and blue of the sky is reflected in the water. Manet enjoyed painting pictures of the sea during his holidays; some of his ancestors had been sailors.

Although he never went all the way with the Impressionists, especially in their treatment of light, Manet was very interested in the work of these young artists. He used to join them every week for discussions at the Café Guerbois in the Rue Clichy; Monet, Renoir, Degas and the others all admired him for his modern ideas on art; in fact they were laughingly nicknamed, "Manet's Gang". He came closest to them in some of his later open-air pictures like "A Corner of the Bellevue Garden" with its light touches of colour, and the delightful picture called "The Laundress" in which a small boy watches his mother hanging out the clothes to dry. He uses an impressionist technique too in his very fine portrait of his friend the writer Stéphane Mallarmé, with its thick, rapid brushstrokes.

Among his pictures of Parisian life, Manet included several scenes in cafés and bars, subjects like "La Serveuse de Bocks" (The Waitress) painted in 1871, of which one version is in the National Gallery, and a better one in the Louvre. The best picture of this kind is the brilliant

MANET   *Collection Payne Bingham, New York*

LE PRINTEMPS

Spring

and original composition, "A Bar at the Folies-Bergère" which was painted for the Salon in 1881 and is in the Courtauld Institute. The central figure, a rather bored looking waitress, stands at her counter; behind her is a mirror which reflects not only her own back and the customer she is serving, but also the ladies and gentlemen in the restaurant. The objects on the counter, the bottles each with its label, a bowl of oranges and two pink roses in a vase, make a charming still life picture on their own account. The waitress appears again in an attractive pastel portrait in the Museum at Dijon, in which she is wearing a blue costume and smart hat with a turned up brim.

While he was still comparatively young, Manet was stricken by a disease which slowly paralysed him. The "Folies-Bergère" was his last large picture; afterwards he was obliged to confine himself to small still life paintings and portraits, mostly in pastel. He also produced some engravings. One of the most delightful of his late works is the portrait of a young girl, called "Le Printemps" (Spring) on p. 117.

At the end of his life, Manet was officially honoured for his work and was made a Chevalier of the Legion of Honour in 1881. Two years later, at the age of fifty-one, he died.

Manet is an attractive, as well as an important figure in the history of art. Handsome in appearance, courteous in manner and fond of social life he made many friends. He was enthusiastic about his work and loved the very act of painting. To-day his pictures fetch fantastic prices whenever they come on the market. They are valuable not only for themselves as works of art, but also for the fascinating glimpses in them of the city of Paris and the people who lived there a hundred years ago.

MANET   *National Gallery, London*
MUSIC IN THE TUILERIES GARDENS
This picture contains many portraits: The handsome figure on the extreme left is Manet; the little man with glasses sitting under a tree is Offenbach, the famous composer of 'Tales of Hoffmann' and 'Orpheus in the Underworld'; the two ladies in identical yellow costumes and blue bonnets are well-known society ladies.

MANET STILL LIFE WITH FRUIT *Louvre, Paris*

MANET MUSIC IN THE TUILERIES GARDENS *National Gallery, London*

GALLERIES, MUSEUMS AND CHURCHES
With abbreviations used

AUSTRIA

Vienna — Albertina (drawings)
Kunsthistorisches *Kuns*

BELGIUM

Antwerp — Cathedral
Royal Museum of Fine Arts
Bruges — Municipal Museum
Brussels — Royal Museum of Fine Arts
Ghent — St Bavon Cathedral
DENMARK — Copenhagen Glyptotek
FRANCE
Dijon — Magnin Museum
Nancy — Museum
Paris — Louvre

GERMANY
Berlin — Gallery
Cassel — Gallery
Cologne — Museum
Dresden — Gallery
Mannheim — Kunsthalle *Kunst.*
Munich — Pinakothek *Pina.*

**GREAT
BRITAIN**
Edinburgh — National Gallery of
Scotland *N.G.S.*
London — British Museum *B.M.*
Courtauld Institute
Dulwich Art Gallery
National Gallery *Nat. Gal.*
Royal Academy *R.A.*
Tate Gallery
Victoria & Albert Museum
V.& A.
Wallace Collection *Wall.*
Wellington Museum
Well M.

HOLLAND
Amsterdam — Rijksmuseum *Rijks.*
The Six Collection
The Hague — Mauritshuis *Maur.*
Rotterdam — Boymans Museum
M. van der Vorm Museum

ITALY

Assisi — Upper and Lower Churches
of St Francis
Florence — Church of S. Croce
Pitti Palace
Uffizi Gallery
S. Marco
Milan — Brera Gallery
Padua — S. Maria dell'Arena
S. Maria delle Grazie
Rome — Borghese Gallery *Borgh.*
Doria Palace
Farnesina Palace
Vatican — Pinacoteca
Sistine Chapel
Stanze
Venice — Academy
S. Maria de Firari

**LIECHTEN-
STEIN** — Gallery

SPAIN
Madrid — Escorial
Prado
S. Domingo el Antiguo
Toledo — Cathedral
Church of San Tomé
El Greco Museum
San Vincente Museum

U.S.A.
Cambridge,
Mass. — Fogg Museum
Chicago — Art Institute
Los Angeles — Museum of Fine Arts
Minneapolis — Art Institute
New York — Frick Collection
Metropolitan Museum
of Art *Met.*
Washington — National Gallery of Art
Wash.

U.S.S.R.
Leningrad — Hermitage

Index to Pictures

Page nos. in bold indicate reproductions.
Engravings, Frescoes and Sculpture listed separately at end.